HARVEST MAINE

Autumn Traditions & Fall Flavors

CRYSTAL WARD KENT

Published by American Palate
A Division of The History Press
Charleston, SC 29403
www.historypress.net

First published 2014

Manufactured in the United States

ISBN 978.1.62619.424.3

Library of Congress CIP data applied for.

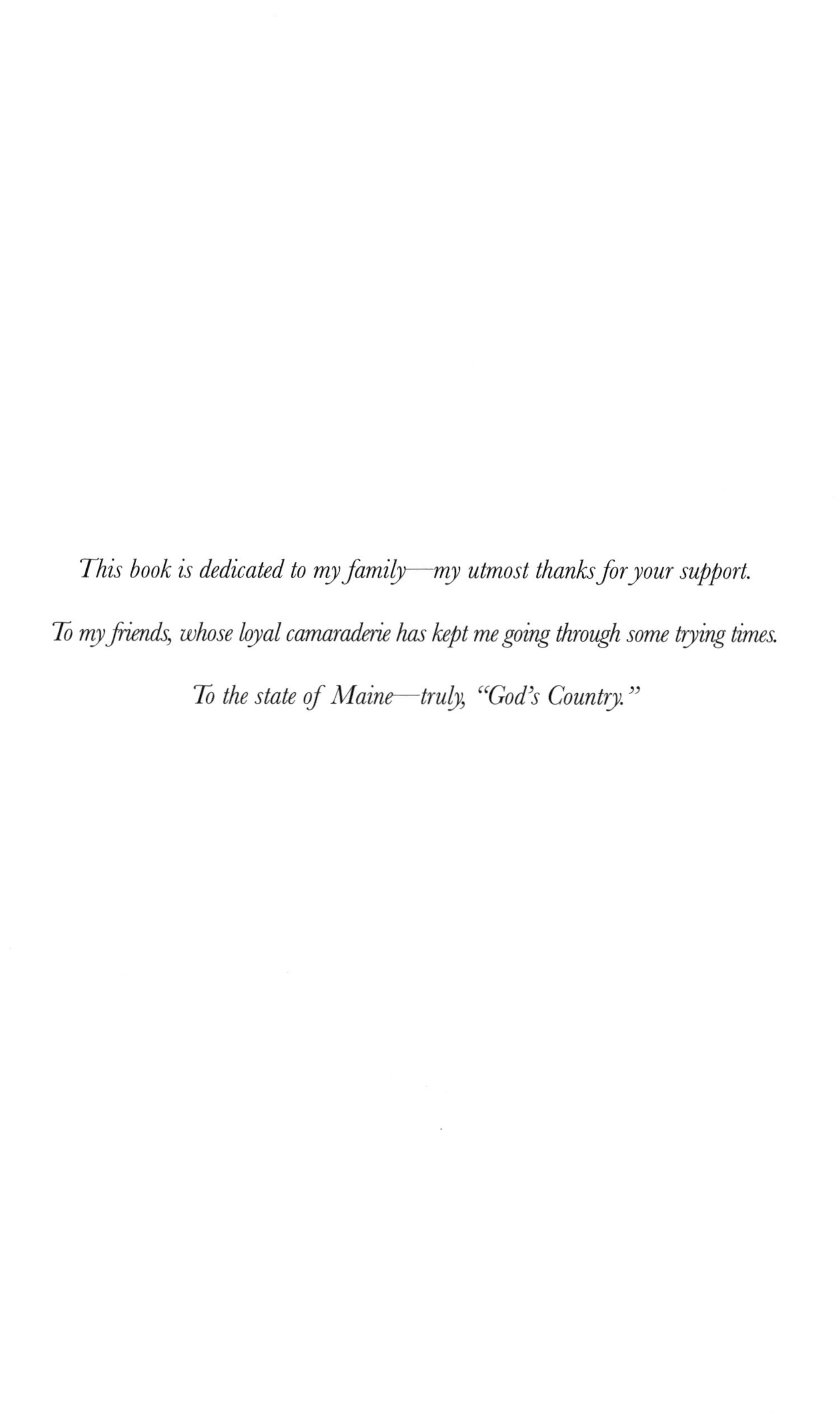

This book is dedicated to my family—my utmost thanks for your support.

To my friends, whose loyal camaraderie has kept me going through some trying times.

To the state of Maine—truly, "God's Country."

CONTENTS

Acknowledgements

Special thanks to all who helped with this book, most notably Marcia Peverly and Budd Perry for providing wonderful photography; Dr. Diane H. Ranes PhD and Ronn Orenstein Photography for fabulous photos of the Damariscotta Pumpkinfest; and Robin Mayer, Pumpkinfest coordinator, for her extensive assistance. Thanks also to Paul Fuller, of Eastern Fishing & Outdoor Expositions and *Bird Dogs Afield TV*, and Cyrus Morgan for their assistance with my hunting questions.

Chapter 1

Autumn Comes to Maine

You see the first signs in August—a touch of red on a maple, a bit of flame edging the leaves of a sumac. The nights take on a chillier feel, hinting at cooler times ahead, while in the fields, the whir of summer insects rises to a crescendo as they pour out one last song before their final sleep.

By September, there is no denying that summer is on the wane. Apple trees and sickle pears hang heavy with fruit. Deer and other wildlife steal into the orchards at dawn and dusk, seeking the drops. Along the old stone walls, grapevines burst with deep purple bounty, and birds, squirrels and chipmunks race to see who can devour the most.

Mornings are quiet now, as summer's trilling birdsong is replaced by the winter calls of blue jays and nuthatches, chickadees and titmice. Gone are the colorful birds of summer, already wending their way to warmer climes. Instead, flocks of sparrows in endless patterns of brown and gray huddle in the bushes. These hardy species will ride out the snow and cold, feeding on winter berries and seeds.

For some time now, the call of wild geese has been heard in the evening. As moonlight floods the cold, clear skies, long skeins can be seen embarking on their ageless journey to southern fields. Their haunting call has a sadness to it—a farewell to summer, to the year nearly spent.

As September deepens, the trees begin their color show. Maples put on the most vibrant display, with leaves that turn scarlet and orange, gold and yellow, sometimes all in one leaf. Oaks add flair with tones ranging from the vibrant red of scrub oaks to yellows and rich browns. Beeches, birches,

A stormy autumn sky forms a dramatic backdrop to a windy Maine hillside. *Marcia Peverly photo.*

aspens and ashes bring splashes of gold, while bushes and shrubs such as sumac, blueberry and barberry provide a riot of red.

Maine is two-thirds forested, and much of the state's woodlands include conifers such as pine, spruce and balsam, but the evergreens only enhance the hardwoods' colorful display, their dark green foliage adding dramatic contrast to the flaming tones around them. The state's abundant lakes and ponds create numerous picturesque views as autumn's colors are mirrored in the dark blue waters.

Even along the coast, brilliant foliage is seen, and the autumn panorama is enhanced by the amber waves of the marsh grasses that stretch to the ocean beyond. The coast casts a different spell in fall. Gone are the tourists with their colorful umbrellas, beach towels and coolers. Now, the shore belongs to wind and water, sand and rock. Offshore storms send strong winds and surging tides sweeping in. The beaches become a treasure-trove of shells and sea glass polished by the pounding waves. A few hardy souls stroll the shore, invigorated by the wind, the ocean's roar and having this wild world to themselves.

Fall brings not only storms but also cold air sweeping down from Canada. Nothing is more striking than the dramatic skyscapes formed by an arriving cold front. Row upon row of dark blue clouds reach back to the northern mountains. They float in low and ominous, their shadowed undersides promising cold and wind and hinting of the winter to come. Suddenly, a shaft of sunlight breaks through the dark ranks, burnishing the foliage below and backlighting the landscape so gilded trees glow against the slate blue of cloud. It is dramatic and beautiful, the juxtaposition of one season on the wane against another's advent.

As October progresses, early morning frost is already riming the fields. The harvest is well in, save for a few late root crops, and farm festivals are in full swing. Much of Maine is farmland, although not the large-scale ventures of the Midwest. Maine farming tends to be smaller scale—apple farms and dairies, vegetable farms or a bit of everything. Up north, in the broad, flat land known as "the County," large tracts are devoted to potato farming, one of the state's major industries, but smaller growers are found everywhere. On a crisp fall weekend, families need not travel far to come upon a farm stand or pick-your-own operation. Here, they take a hayride into the fields, eager to gather pumpkins or apples. Later, back at the farm, they may sample homemade cider and doughnuts, enjoy some fiddle music or simply relish being out on a brisk fall day. They know the days of being able to sit and linger are drawing to an end. Winter is closing in, and every picnic and excursion is savored.

By late October, snow will already have brushed the mountains and sometimes even the entire state. Many of the leaves will be down, but the rusty brown foliage of certain oaks will cling well into the winter. Halloween will bring costumed children to the door, although often with ski jackets over their attire. More than once, a light snowstorm has brought a trick instead of a treat!

Night falls early now, with the last gleam of sunset fading around suppertime. A cool wind rises, rustling the last leaves and rattling the tree branches. The smell of wood smoke floats on the air, and somewhere an owl hoots as it soars off on its nightly hunt. A night like this calls for hearty, comforting food—chowders and stews, a plate of baked beans with homemade bread, a cheesy casserole. Surely there will be pie for dessert—apple or pumpkin, mincemeat or squash—something that reflects the season's bounty. With the last sweet bite lingering on the tongue, families welcome the evening to come. How good to be snug inside, full and warm, savoring the season as autumn comes to Maine.

Chapter 2

FAIR SEASON

As August fades into September, the bounty of Maine's harvest begins. Fields are ripe with late corn; pumpkins, squash and gourds fatten on the vines. The last of the tomatoes, cucumbers and pole beans are ready for canning, capturing those juicy bites of summer in a jar. Fruit crops are ready, too. Late blueberries and raspberries are quickly gathered, and the orchards are heavy with fruit.

After a summer of grazing on good grass, livestock are sleek and handsome. The morning chill gives friskiness to their step, or maybe it is excitement for the season ahead—not just the season of autumn but also fair season.

There are not as many farmers in Maine as there once were, but the state is still largely rural, and farmer or not, everyone welcomes fair season. A country fair brings a touch of magic to Maine's small towns. There is the excitement of the setup crews arriving and then the big trucks bringing the rides, followed by the parade of food vendors—French fries and fried dough, corn dogs and sausages. The farmers come soon after, trundling in horses and cattle of every shape and size, along with pigs, chicken, sheep and goats, with maybe a burro or alpaca or two. The fairground barns are suddenly full of animals and tack, food and buckets, with families bustling about making their hoofed charges beautiful. The fields around the fairground become a city of RVs and pickup trucks. Lawn chairs and tables appear; a radio plays. People sit outside and play cards or eat supper. A little community forms. Finally, all is ready. The tents are up, their colorful pennants flying in the wind. The lights are strung, a switch is thrown and presto! Magic appears in the warm autumn night. Everything is color and sound, from the swirling lights of the amusement rides to the tinny music of the merry-go-round. The cry of the barkers on the Midway mingles with the roar of the crowd from the competition rings and the low of cattle in nearby barns. Even the air has a unique aroma as the tempting smells of popcorn and fried dough blend with the earthier ones of manure and hay.

The harvest is celebrated across the length and breadth of Maine—from the small Acton Fair in York County to Presque Isle's State Fair in Maine's far north. The Skowhegan Fair claims to be Maine's oldest continuously running fair, having begun in 1818, but perhaps the state's most famous fair is Fryeburg, which typically runs the last weekend in September through the first weekend in October. More than 300,000 visitors flock to the Fryeburg Fair during its run. Set in a region of unparalleled beauty high in Maine's western mountains, the fair rewards visitors with spectacular foliage as well as a good time. Fairgoers have been flocking to the Fryeburg region for well over a century. The West Oxford Agricultural Society, which presents the Fryeburg Fair, was incorporated on June 3, 1851. Originally, only nine Maine towns were included, but six New Hampshire towns later joined in 1888. After moving the fair from town to town for the first few years, the society purchased the 26-acre location for $133 in 1885. Over the last one hundred years, the fair site has expanded to 180 acres and includes one hundred permanent buildings with more than three thousand camping sites. During the fair's run, these will quickly fill up.

The parking area is rimmed by tall pine trees, which are also sprinkled throughout the fairgrounds proper. Inside the gate, the Ferris wheel rises over a sea of tents, trailers, buildings and corrals. The fair offers something for all ages, including the livestock shows. From miniature horses to the giant draft breeds, from dairy cows to beef stock and from sheep to goats, the best and brightest of each species will parade into the ring, brushed and ribboned, sometimes led by small children and other times by teens or adults. Today, there is a contest to evaluate good breeding stock. Lithe young women in dark slacks and crisp white shirts wrangle horses four times their size as a group of Shires is brought into the ring. Shires are an English draft horse breed dating back to the tenth century; knights of old rode these mighty steeds, and they retain a royal look with their fine arched necks and shiny coats. Although Shires come in gray and bay colors, the classic Shires are black with white blazes and fetlocks, and it is this type that is being judged now.

The judges are looking to see how well the breed's notable characteristics are being passed from dam to foal. As a result, both mothers and foals are shepherded in for review. The foals are nervous, not used to the crowds. They try to duck behind their mothers. When the pair is asked to demonstrate their gait, several foals try to break into exuberant gallops. But in each case, their young female handlers, undaunted at dealing with animals the size of small cars (Shires can weigh over a ton), quickly calm them down, restoring their conformation as they pass in review.

Outside, Belted Galloways, nicknamed the "Oreo cows" because they are black on the head, shoulders and rump but banded with white around their middles, await their turn to be shown. They are wrapped in cellophane to protect them from any stray mud splatters, making them appear to have just come from a bovine spa.

Meanwhile, in the far outside show ring, show jumping has commenced. The crowd is hushed as each long-limbed hunter enters the arena and the rider begins guiding the horse over the myriad jumps. Horse and rider move as one; just a touch on the neck or a press on the flank tells the horse where to go and at what pace. Pole jumps, low walls, open pits, brush jumps—the

A miniature horse, mascot of its owner's farm, waits his turn to be shown at the Fryeburg Fair. *Crystal Kent photo.*

pair flies over each obstacle, receiving applause for a job well done after a clean round.

Show jumpers are masters of precision, and in a different sense, so are border collies. At the sheep-herding demonstrations, they are blurs of movement as they expertly dart in and around the wayward flock, directing them where the shepherd wants with well-placed nips and nudges. At times, the dogs are almost belly to the ground as they creep up on laggards and then, with a quick nip or burst of speed, urge them back to the flock. Sometimes, the shepherd asks the dog to cut out just one or two sheep and bring them round, and the dog does so, deftly separating his target(s) from the group. The entire exercise is done in near silence, save for the baas of the sheep. The dog neither yips nor barks, and the shepherd communicates with the dog with hand signals or a few pipes on his whistle. The dogs are equally adept at herding goats and cows, and it is clear that they love to work.

Sheep farmers will tell you that it takes about two years for a herding dog to be able to competently work a flock of adult animals. Shepherds start the puppies with small, easier-to-manage animals such as ducklings. The young dogs then work up to adult birds, then lambs and then adult sheep. Putting a puppy in with a large animal is a recipe for disaster, as the dog may be terrified for life if he has a bad experience. Herding can be dangerous work for an inexperienced dog, as sheep and cattle can kick and butt, and real injury is possible. Phased-in training allows the dog to learn how animals react before adult livestock are being worked. Training sessions may take place every day and are kept short so the dog does not feel overwhelmed. At the end of each session, the shepherd rewards the dog with playtime—fetching a ball or some other activity he enjoys. The dogs are not taught how to herd—this is instinctive. Instead, they are taught how to use that instinct to do what the shepherd wants: bring the flock to the fields or back to the shepherd, drive the flock through obstacles such as gates and urge the flock into pens. When the shepherd wants the dog to stop herding, he tells it to lie down. The dog does so but never takes his eyes off the flock. Herding dogs, especially border collies, have laser-like focus when it comes to watching the flocks. They will not move a muscle while on the job.

One shepherd told me that the secret to a good herding dog is in the stare: "A good dog can make those sheep behave with a look!"

At the other end of the fair entertainment spectrum is the pig scramble. There are no deft maneuvers here, just every child—and pig—for himself! Controlled mayhem is what happens when squealing young pigs and eager children are turned loose in a corral. The goal is for the children to catch the pigs; if they catch one, they can raise it to show at the next year's fair. However, grabbing a fast, agile, slippery piglet is much easier said then done. Pigs are racing, darting, oinking; children are running, falling, laughing, hollering; and the crowd is roaring at the antics. Eventually, by some minor miracle, bedraggled, dusty children will emerge with piglets in tow, but only after several minutes of complete chaos.

Among the more esoteric events featured at the fair is the skillet toss. Every woman who has had to cook for a demanding family has probably at one time had the urge to heave her frying pan across the room. After the umpteenth query of "What's for dinner?" or complaints about what is being served, what joy to take that fry pan and toss it out the window! Well, at the Fryeburg Fair, women can throw their skillets as far as they want—and maybe win a prize for doing so. Contestants compete by age group, and skillets are provided by the fair. Would-be competitors are urged to start practicing now, and next fall could see their frying pans flying the farthest!

Nearby, the big draft horses get ready to pull sledges of ever-increasing weight as they vie for the top prize. Their manes and tails are done up with braids and plumes, and the just-brushed feathers around their big hooves

A Belgian draft horse is led across the Fryeburg fairgrounds. Draft horses are judged on conformation and breeding, and some also compete at pulling sledges. *Marcia Peverly photo.*

flutter with each movement. The horses know they are on display and prance a little as they come into the shoot. Their harnesses jingle, and they give little huffs of excitement. Their handler quickly hooks them to the sledge, then instantly urges them to "Get up! Get up!" They do, haunches straining, necks arched, pulling the massive load as far as they can down the stretch. Many are matched pairs—handsome Percherons, Clydesdales and Shires with coats of burnished gold, chestnut or black. These are time-honored breeds whose work was once essential to the hard chores of farm life—the planting, the hauling of timber, the moving of huge wagons of goods. Today, as they compete, they pay tribute to this heritage, to the days when man and horse worked as one.

Not all the fair competition takes place in the show ring; much of it is of the quieter variety as crafters, growers and bakers are judged on everything from the quality of their pies to the size of their squashes, the sweetness of their jams and the deftness of the stitches on their quilts. The quality of these items highlights the depth of Maine's rural roots. There is still pride in doing things by hand, in taking the time to roll out pie crust, piece a quilt, plant a garden. Doing by hand is also still a necessity in much of Maine, as incomes are often strained, and "making do" is as much a way of life as lobstering, farming, fishing or logging.

After rounds of rides and activities, it is time for a look at exhibits and items for sale, as well as mouth-watering fair food. Each year, the fair hosts exhibits of antique wagons and sleighs. The elaborately carved gypsy wagons are among the most eye-catching and are true works of art with their colors and intricate detailing. Also fascinating are the displays of Maine's gemstones and minerals; the western part of the state is a treasure-trove of tourmaline, garnets and quartz, and gorgeous samples of these and many other varieties are worth a look. Various conservation societies highlight their work to preserve Maine's wild lands, and the Maine Department of Inland Fisheries & Wildlife has arranged for a jaw-dropping exhibit of two adult bull moose locked in mortal combat. Provided by New Hampshire Fish & Game and called "Forever Locked: The Battling Bull Moose of Fowlertown," the life-size taxidermy display showcases two moose that fought to the death when their antlers became entangled. While hunting on October 9, 2003, Ray Deragon of New Hampshire found the carcasses of two bull moose near Sunapee Mountain. A closer look showed that the moose's antlers were still locked together. It is not uncommon for moose to fight during the rutting season as they vie for breeding privileges with cows. These moose died of stress, starvation and dehydration after their antlers became caught in such

The balloon man at the Fryeburg Fair, 1937. *Photo by George French, courtesy of the Maine State Archives.*

a way that they could not break free. Deragon contacted local conservation officer John Wimsatt, who believed that such a natural phenomenon would make an interesting educational exhibit. They photographed the moose as

A farmer stacks pumpkins in Fryeburg, 1941. *Photo by George French, courtesy of the Maine State Archives.*

they lay and then carefully removed the carcasses. A campaign was launched, and volunteers raised $400,000 to complete the exhibit.

"Forever Locked" draws gasps wherever it appears. Both moose were huge, and each had large racks; one had a rack, or antler display, of fifty-three inches, and the other's rack was sixty-one inches—nearly five feet wide! The moose antlers in the display are the originals and have never been unlocked since they were found. The skins on the moose were provided by local moose hunters since the originals were too badly decomposed.

No one can attend the fair without trying the Midway. Here, tiers of stuffed animals bump up against huge bundles of balloons and all those "must-have" prizes that lure us to "take a chance." The barkers urge us on—throw a ball or dart, squirt a water pistol, shoot a pop gun, place your bet, it's all in fun! You could win a prize! And if Lady Luck does not favor you, there is still plenty to eat. Popcorn, peanuts, hot dogs, burgers, pizza, funnel cakes, cotton candy—all the classics are here. But so are clam chowder, baked beans, lobster rolls, maple sugar and Moxie—it is Maine, after all.

Shopping is eclectic, from new types of garden hoses and electric fireplaces to T-shirts and jewelry; homemade jams, jellies and beef jerky; and "swornby" mole repellant. Almost everyone goes home with at least one classic item and one of the "What was I thinking?" variety.

Most of the fair's attendees come for fun, but the fair actually serves multiple purposes. It is a unique blend of entertainment, education and economic engine. The Fryeburg Fair brings a huge amount of business to this rural section of western Maine, and for the farmers and vendors showcased at the event, it brings the opportunity for new connections, new customers and new income.

Fairs are also agricultural expos, providing the latest updates on new technology, products and technique. Some of the top minds in the region offer presentations and chances to share information during the fair's run. Everyone from the full-time grower to the backyard gardener has the opportunity to pick up useful information and gain additional resources.

The sun is setting now, and the fairgrounds are agleam with colored lights. A country-western band is tuning up, and before long folks will be dancing till the wee hours. A fresh crowd of people is streaming through the gates, eager to try the rides, hear the band and watch the closing fireworks. Other families are heading home; little ones, half asleep, are slung over shoulders, stuffed animals clenched in hands, a lone balloon floating out behind them. Filling their heads are sweet dreams of the fair, of that touch of magic on a warm autumn night.

Chapter 3

It's the Great Pumpkin, Charlie Brown!

Among the crops being judged at fall fairs are pumpkins, especially giant pumpkins—in fact, the bigger the better. Giant pumpkins have attracted a huge following and seem to inspire otherwise normal people to strange flights of fancy. Perhaps nowhere is that in more evidence than at the Damariscotta Pumpkin Festival.

For those who live near Damariscotta, Maine, and have grown a giant pumpkin, there is only one thing to do: turn it into a boat and race it on the Damariscotta River! For the past seven years, this small town has hosted an annual Pumpkinfest celebrating giant pumpkins. It started as an informal gathering of a few friends but turned into a major town activity attracting more than ten thousand people over three days. Pumpkinfest now includes a giant weigh off with $10,000 in cash prizes, pumpkin boat racing, a pumpkin derby and a pumpkin drop, where giant pumpkins are dropped from a crane two hundred feet in the air onto junked cars. The pumpkin boat races are a huge draw, as pumpkins do not steer very well, tend to ride low in the water and can be tricky when it comes to launching or disembarking. Pumpkinfest is usually held October 1–10 for those who want to check out the fun (or madness). Other pumpkin activities involve using catapults to launch huge squash incredible distances. Amazingly, there are entire web pages devoted to instructions on how to build these devices. Safety glasses are advised!

Carving pumpkins into intricate designs is not new, but carving them under water is unique. At the festival, teams of scuba divers from OceansWide plunge into the harbor for the sole purpose of holding a giant pumpkin in

The Pumpkin Derby at the Damariscotta Pumpkinfest. These little race "cars" are actually decorated pumpkins that have been fitted with wheels. *Ronn Orenstein Photography.*

Pumpkin boats get ready to launch during the regatta portion of the Damariscotta Pumpkinfest. *Ronn Orenstein Photography.*

place while another diver carves the pumpkin. (If the pumpkins were not held in place, they would pop to the surface like giant orange beach balls.) OceansWide's ROUS (Remotely Operated Unmanned Submersible), which is controlled from the surface, broadcasts live streaming video of the carving to crowds gathered on shore.

At Pumpkinfest, kids get into the act thanks to the Pumpkin Derby (think Pinewood Derby with pumpkins). Yes, take a small pumpkin, thread two axles through it and attach wheels—now it is ready to roll! Competing pumpkins can be hollowed out but must retain their pumpkin shape, and racers—including axles, wheels and decorations—cannot exceed twenty pounds. (Entries are weighed before racing.) Specially trained officials also examine the racers to make sure that there are no "cheater pumpkins"—i.e. watermelons, gourds or other squash masquerading as pumpkins.

In a more traditional vein, the festival also features pumpkin dessert-making and pie-eating contests, plus displays of carved and painted pumpkins. The artistry in the pumpkin creations is incredible. These are not just variations on grinning jack o' lanterns but pumpkins transformed into unbelievable creations. Previous transformations have included a mouse with cheese, numerous kinds of monsters, a mammoth cheeseburger, a giant strawberry, a car, a bat and a teapot. Visit www.damariscottapumpkinfest.com to see previous years' artistry. While pumpkin-related activities are the main theme, the event also offers street performers and musical entertainment, lots of great food and a "Zombie Run" road race.

A bit of background about giant pumpkins: Pumpkins are one of autumn's most charming and versatile fruits (yes, they really are fruits, not vegetables). They are typically pictured demurely decorating porch railings or tucked cleverly into fall displays. The small, sweet pie pumpkins conjure up images of tasty creations decked with whipped cream. But as Pumpkinfest shows, there is another side to pumpkins—a monster side! These are behemoths of the field that have to be lifted by a team of weightlifters or a crane and trundled into town on flatbeds. These massive gourds frequently weigh in at eight hundred, nine hundred or more than one thousand pounds. That's a lot of pie!

According to "Backyard Gardener" writer Don Langevin, as recently as sixteen years ago, the heaviest (official) pumpkin weighed in at a mere 403 pounds. Since then, the record has been shattered again and again, largely due to the research of one man, the late Howard Dill of Windsor, Nova Scotia. Dill's family has farmed for five generations, and all his life, he was fascinated by pumpkins. His quest to grow ever-bigger pumpkins led him to teach himself the basics of plant genetics, and in 1979, Dill grew the first

Massive pumpkins are turned into works of art each year at the Damariscotta Pumpkinfest. A wide range of carving tools, household tools, paints and "accessories" are used to create designs that range from realistic to fanciful. *Ronn Orenstein Photography.*

pumpkin to break the 400-pound barrier, setting a world record. For the next four years, he held the world record and missed hitting it a fifth time by just 5 pounds. Giant pumpkin fans sought out his seeds, and Dill's Atlantic Giant, the premier seed for growing enormous pumpkins, was soon patented. It remains the seed of choice if you wish to grow 'em big.

Consider the giant pumpkin: The second largest in the world in 1994 had a girth of 176 inches. That's more than 14.5 feet around! Small children,

"Monster" pumpkins are hauled in on flatbed trucks at the Damariscotta Pumpkinfest. They will be weighed and judged, and some will be hoisted up in the air by cranes and then dropped onto old trucks. *Dr. Diane H. Ranes PhD photo.*

even families, can fit inside these gargantuan gourds. The year 1996 saw the "birth" of the first 1,000-pound pumpkin. One Atlantic Giant was consumed in the form of 442 pies—they were sold for five dollars each, with the proceeds going to charity. A few years back, at the Topsfield Fair in Topsfield, Massachusetts, it took twelve men to roll a 914-pound pumpkin onto the scale. But perhaps the most humorous tale was of one of Dill's Giants that was shipped from Nova Scotia to Chicago. Dill built his own heavy-duty crate to ensure the pumpkin's safe arrival, but this time, such a large container raised concerns. The box took four hours to clear customs, as drug enforcement agents were called in. Officials refused to believe that a box that large contained a pumpkin.

The 2010 world champ weighed in at 1,810.5 pounds and was grown by Chris Stevens of New Richmond, Wisconsin. Back in 2002, the world record holder was Charlie Houghton, of New Hampshire, who grew a 1,337.6-pounder. So far, most of the champions have been raised from Atlantic Giant seeds, which made Dill proud.

GROWING A MONSTER PUMPKIN

* Start with good seed, such as Atlantic Giant. Most of the recent champions have been this variety.
* Get your soil tested. According to Howard Dill, the big ones like soil with a pH ranging from 6.5 to 7. Add whatever additions the soil test recommends, as well as plenty of organic matter such as composted manure—cow or horse is best.
* Giants take 130 days to mature, so plan to sow accordingly. In northern climates, where giant pumpkins do best, you will need to start your seed indoors about four weeks before the last frost date.
* Transplant to outside once the frost threat is gone. Keep at least twenty-five to thirty-five feet between the plants so the vines have room to grow.
* Giant pumpkins can put on fifteen to twenty pounds *per day*, so water every day or two—you need a good, strong plant to sustain tremendous fruit growth.
* Once you have vines producing, you'll need to trim, selecting only the strongest vines for nurturing. As the vines produce multiple pumpkins, you'll need to choose the pumpkin with the best growth to bring along.
* Feed wisely! Feed once or twice per week over the entire plant area, using a water-soluble fertilizer. Be careful not to overfeed—if pumpkins start growing too fast, Langevin says they can "literally tear themselves from the vine and explode."

THE MONSTER PUMPKIN CAPER

I should confess that while I have never grown a true giant, a large pumpkin incident does lurk in my family history. I do not know what triggered our Big Pumpkin Caper. Frustration? Retaliation? Justice? For years, we had patiently carved jack o' lanterns, only to see them stolen and smashed on Halloween Eve. One moment they were happily glowing; the next, they were a sodden mass in the road.

We tried tucking them under the bushes at night, but too often the thieves beat us to it, and forgoing pumpkins was not an option. What was Halloween without pumpkins?

My father, who has always had the kind of creative, devious mind that kids love and teachers fear, had an idea. "What if we booby trapped one?" he said. "What if we got the biggest, most tempting pumpkin and rigged it to scare the pants off of anyone who touched it?" For a wild moment, my mother had visions of exploding pumpkins, but once Dad reassured her that C-4 wasn't involved, everyone was on board.

The first stop was Applecrest Farm. There, we selected the largest pumpkin we could lift. The one-hundred-pound monster had "steal me" written all over it. We rolled it into the car, and the plotting began. Some combination of light and sound was needed. We wanted all would-be thieves to be lit up like daylight, and we needed sound to alert us that a pumpkin thief was on the premises. After all, no one wanted to miss the fun.

My dad disappeared into his workshop for several days. Our neighbor got into the act, and by week's end, the perfect plan was hatched. Wires were run from the front steps to nearby bushes and then concealed with leaves. The pumpkin was groomed for its starring role. Carved and lit, its eerie Halloween smile was a mask for the deviltry it concealed. On trick-or-treat night, the jack o' lantern was placed on a pressure switch. As long as the pumpkin was in place, nothing happened. But the minute its weight was lifted, two floodlights, hidden in nearby evergreens, lit up the steps. At the same time, a submarine dive horn blasted "Arooga, Arooga! DIVE! DIVE!" at top volume. The horn came courtesy of our helpful neighbor, a former chief in the U.S. Navy.

Trick-or-treaters came and went for several hours, and all was quiet. Then, about 9:00 p.m., the horn sounded—along with screaming. A teenage girl was dancing around on the front walk, yelling her head off. We rushed out, and after my father silenced the horn, she quieted down. Everyone had a good laugh; she apologized and then made her escape. A few minutes later, the alarm sounded again. We heard a pickup truck roar away and glimpsed two long white legs dive into the back. The pumpkin was left rocking on the steps. Four more times the alarm blasted, and each time the pumpkin was left unscathed while the would-be thieves stood paralyzed on the lawn. "What scared you the most?" my dad eagerly asked one teen. "The lights," he said. "Man, they were like two big eyes just bursting out of the bushes at you!" Ultimately, the evening turned into a fanfest, with the teenagers fascinated by the booby trap and my dad basking in the feedback on his creation.

Needless to say, the whole neighborhood was aware of the caper, given the fact that a submarine dive horn was sounding every half hour, lights were blazing and a whole lot of screaming was going on. Since this was not a regular occurrence, no one complained. In fact, most paid their respects to my dad. Thanks to his booby trap, not one pumpkin was stolen that year. Clearly, ours was a neighborhood where the pumpkins were fighting back!

MORE ABOUT MAINE

Growing a Giant: If you are a giant pumpkin fan, be advised that most of the champions have been raised in small backyard gardens. For more detailed instructions, visit Don Langevin's excellent instructions at www.backyardgardener.com/wcgp/tips/10 steps.html or check out his book *How-to-Grow World Class Giant Pumpkins* from Annedawn Publishing.

Giant Pumpkin Weigh-Offs: Giant pumpkin weigh-offs are held annually on the first Saturday in October at various locations around the United States and Canada. Check out the Pumpkin Patch website at www.backyardgardener.com/gpc.html.

Chapter 4

Maine Outdoors

The summit of Mount Agamenticus in York, Maine, overlooks a vast panorama of fall countryside. Woodlands, vivid with fall color, stretch for miles in three directions. Here and there, one sees a house, a church steeple, a ribbon of road, but for the most part, the land appears undisturbed. Glistening ponds and the shimmer of rivers winding to the sea add splashes of blue amid the scarlet and gold of the forest. Far to the northwest lie the rugged outlines of New Hampshire's Presidential Range. Mount Washington, already snow-capped, immediately draws the eye. To the east, the view is equally spectacular, for here the ocean reaches in one broad expanse to the horizon. Along the rim of coastline, small villages dot the shore—Ogunquit and Wells, Arundel and the Kennebunks. Off Cape Neddick, Nubble Light stands like a sentinel on its rocky island. For more than a century, it has warned mariners during storms and fog of the danger hidden beneath the crashing waves.

Mount Agamenticus is not a tall mountain; it rises a mere 692 feet, but that is enough to make it the highest peak in York County. Visitors can drive to the summit or choose to hike any of the numerous trails winding up the mountain. Back in the 1950s and '60s, Mount Aggie (as the locals call it) was a ski area, complete with rope tow and lodge. Remnants of those skiing days still remain in the form of old winches, poles and partially grown-over ski runs. The lodge has been converted to a nature education and visitors' center. A consortium of local towns (York and South Berwick), the Nature Conservancy, the Maine Department of Inland Fisheries & Wildlife and the

The view from Mount Agamenticus in York, Maine, captures New Hampshire's Presidential Range to the West. *Marcia Peverly photo.*

York Water District care for what is now called the Mount Agamenticus Conservation Region. Thanks to their efforts, more than ten thousand acres around the mountain are now conserved, creating the largest area of undeveloped woodland habitat in New England. This is no small feat, as southern Maine is under significant development pressure, and wild land all too easily disappears.

Surveying these woodlands, it is easy to imagine being a settler from centuries ago. How awe-inspiring to climb this small peak and see such magnificent vistas flowing in every direction. Native Americans already knew Mount Agamenticus as a special place; it was considered home to the spirit gods of the Abenaki tribe. The top of the mountain is also where a pile of stones recognizes St. Aspinquid, spiritual leader of the Abenaki and medicine man to many area tribes. His Native American name was believed to be Passconaway, but it is said that when he converted to Christianity, he was then called St. Aspinquid. When he died at the age of ninety-four in 1682, Native Americans came from hundreds of miles away to pay tribute. Legend has it that thousands of animals were sacrificed here at the summit to honor his memory. As was the custom of his people, his grave was covered with stones. Visitors are still invited to leave stones at the peak in his honor.

Mount Agamenticus is home to abundant wildlife, including deer and bear, fisher cat, bobcat and coyote, raccoon, rabbit, fox and many others. Hawks, eagles, vultures and ravens soar around the summit, riding the thermals and scanning the countryside for prey.

On this fall day, the hawk migration is in full swing. Hundreds of thousands of raptors (hawks, owls, eagles) will leave their North American breeding ranges for wintering grounds in the South, some venturing as far as South America. Hawks come to Mount Agamenticus because it gives them a thermal lift, and they can follow the coastline for guidance on their journey. Late September through mid-October is the best time to watch for hawks, as this time period typically brings northwest winds and clear skies. More than four thousand raptors will pass by each fall, with viewers often seeing hundreds in a day. It starts with the broad wings in September and winds down with the last of the red tails in November. Some birds will stay here, wintering over to hunt across the snow-covered fields, but most journey on. Sharp-shinned hawks, cooper's hawks, northern goshawks, red-shouldered hawks, American kestrels, merlins, ospreys, peregrine falcons, northern harriers and bald eagles are among those wending their way south. These keen-eyed masters of flight captivate the eye as they ride the warm air currents with effortless grace.

V's of geese are also heading southward, their mournful honking drifting back on the breeze. Large flocks will stop at Great Bay and in sheltered coves along the shore to rest and feed before resuming their journey to warmer climates. Autumn is the season of migration, and many species in the animal world are on the move. The primary motivator is the need to find food. When winter's snow and cold halts plant growth and most insects go dormant, those species dependent on these food sources must find new eating spots until spring returns. When the days lengthen, their internal time clocks will again draw them homeward, completing the cycle once more.

Scientists believe that the urge to migrate is embedded in an animals' DNA. They instinctively know when to leave, where to go and when to return. As the days begin to shorten and the first chill sharpens the air, many birds and animals know it is time to begin their annual voyage.

Each fall, hundreds of species and billions of birds pour into the earth's flyways, embarking on journeys their ancestors have taken for centuries. While their destinations may be "pre-programmed," how they find their way is still not fully understood. Research indicates that they may be guided by a combination of things—the position of the sun, the moon and stars; reflected light; the earth's magnetic field; their sense of smell; or geographical landmarks such as rivers and mountain ranges. Yet flocks of birds have been known to navigate across long stretches of featureless ocean, and radar operators have picked up birds flying between cloud layers where they could see neither the sky above nor the land below, and still they reached their destination. How they find their way, year after year, remains both a mystery and a wonder.

The paths of migrants lie in many directions. Earthworms migrate downward, burrowing deeper into the earth's warm soil for the winter and then tunneling up again in the spring. Their journey of roughly fifteen inches coincides perfectly with the return of the spring's songbirds.

Butterflies, seemingly among the most fragile of migrants, also head for warmer destinations. The long-distance champ is the monarch, which journeys from North America to the fir groves of Mexico, a distance of two thousand miles. One of the "jumping-off" points for monarchs is Fort Foster in Kittery Point, Maine. Visitors to the fort around Columbus Day may see hundreds of butterflies, including monarchs and other species, resting on bushes and trees throughout the park. They gain last-minute sustenance from late summer blooms before heading off on their amazing journey.

Even ocean creatures migrate. Sea stars and other marine invertebrates move to deeper waters, leaving their traditional tide pools and shallower habitats. Plankton, perhaps the smallest travelers, migrate to the surface at night and then sink deeper during the day. Larger marine migrants include baleen whales. Humpback whales are a common sight off the Maine coast in summer; our nutrient-rich waters make excellent feeding grounds. But in the fall, the whales leave the cold northern Atlantic for the warm seas of the Caribbean, where they will mate and bear their calves.

The signs of fall can be subtle in the natural world, but they are there. Warm temperatures may linger during the day, fooling us into thinking summer is still here, but a closer look outside shows that autumn has come to Maine. The skeins of geese racing the autumn moon, the tide pools empty of sea stars and urchins and clouds of butterflies on the wing all indicate a change of seasons. Summer is fading to memory, and soon winter will be on our doorstep.

Maine's Fall Color

Few sights are more spectacular than the Maine woods in autumn. The sun streaming through brightly colored leaves makes the trees appear to glow. Maine's abundant hardwoods (deciduous trees that drop their leaves in fall) are aflame with hues ranging from vivid yellows to deepest reds and every shade in between. Scrub oaks flash tones from scarlet to burgundies so deep that they border on black. Sumacs and red maples dazzle with leaves of vermilion, while ashes, beeches and birch flutter leaves of gold. The color show never ceases to cast a spell, but behind the magic, natural science is at work. In fact, the cycle that leads to autumn's foliage spectacle begins in the spring.

The leaves of deciduous trees, such as maples, oaks, beeches and the like, contain pigments. Most dominant is chlorophyll, which gives leaves their basic green color and is tied to a plant's food production. Also present are carotenoids, which produce the yellow, orange and brown colors found in plants. Anthocyanins, the third key pigment, create plants' red hues. Chlorophyll and carotenoids are present in leaf cells throughout the growing season, but most anthocyanins are produced in the autumn. They are a byproduct of excess sugar production in the leaves. During the growing season, chlorophyll is continuously produced and broken down, so leaves appear green. But as the days shorten, chlorophyll production slows and eventually stops. As a result, the carotenoids and anthocyanins that have been present in the leaves all along are now made visible with chlorophyll's absence and the autumn color show begins.

Different tree species turn different hues. Oaks turn red, brown or russet; hickories transform to golden bronze; aspens and ash change to yellow, while dogwoods go a purplish red. The color of maple leaves differs by species, with red maples changing to brilliant scarlet while sugar maples turn to orangey red and black maples turn bright yellow. All hardwoods do not change color at once. Some maples and sumacs may start turning in late August and early September, while oaks are not fully turned until early October or later. And not all trees put on a color display. Evergreens, of course, remain the same, but even among the hardwoods there are exceptions. Elm leaves simply turn brown, wither and fall, creating that classic autumn sound of rustling leaves as they scatter along the roadside.

How brilliant the fall foliage is depends on the weather. Drought conditions in the spring or summer can leave fall soils dry and diminish autumn's colors. A period of unusually warm fall weather can also mute tree color. Fall foliage seems to be best if there has been a wet spring, favorable summer weather and warm, sunny fall days with cool, but not freezing, nights. The warmth of the daytime creates more sugar production in the leaves, which leads to those vivid reds; the cold nights keep the sugars from draining out of the leaves, thus prolonging the brilliant colors.

Because Maine is so heavily forested, seeing its famous fall foliage is easy. From the coast to the mountain ranges of the west and the wilderness of the north, all of Maine's scenery is painted with autumn's brightest brush. In the southern part of the state, head west through apple country along roads such as Route 5, 202 or 11. Farther north, explore the Maine/New Hampshire border on Route 302. This area is known for several covered bridges, the Fryeburg Fair and Sebago Lake. Rock hounds will want to spend time in Oxford County, home to many of Maine's fine gemstones. The western mountains of the Rangeley Lake region offer incredible vistas, as well as the chance to discover waterfalls and sight wildlife such as moose, bear and deer. Vast Moosehead Lake and the Great North Woods not only present stunning autumn vistas but also the chance to see them by canoe, kayak, boat and charter plane. Back on the coast, Acadia National Park juxtaposes autumn color with its dramatic coastline, magnificent views of Bar Harbor from the top of Cadillac Mountain and miles of carriage roads winding through its parkland. North of Bangor lies some of Maine's most rural land, with incredible stretches of fields, forest and distant mountaintops. Seeing the meadows burnished to gold and rimmed by vibrant forest color, with a sweeping expanse of sky overhead, is one of Maine's classic images.

INTO THE WOODS

There is no finer way to appreciate autumn in Maine then to walk through the woods. Gone is summer's heat, and the frozen snows of winter have not yet arrived to make walking difficult. Spring muck and mud (a way of life in Maine!) are also missing, along with that season's ubiquitous black flies. In autumn, there is still warmth, and the trees are in their glory.

Maine's forests are a typical New England mixture of deciduous or leaf-bearing trees, such as maples and oaks, along with conifers, or needle-bearing trees, which include species such as pines, spruces and hemlocks.

No tree captures the essence of Maine more than the eastern white pine. Not only is it the state tree (with the pine cone and tassel being the state's official flower), it also has strong ties to our history. When the settlers first approached the coast of Maine, they were amazed to see great yellow clouds billowing out over the ocean before land was even sighted. These clouds were composed of yellow pine pollen, an indicator of how vast the northern forest was. The settlers did not know it, but they were about to strike gold—the gold of timber like they had never seen before.

White pine built the future and the economy of New England and especially Maine. It built ships, cities and towns. Before the American Revolution, white pine timber was sent over in ever-increasing loads to England and Europe, which were already starved for wood. In fact, in colonial times, the biggest pines were marked "king's pines" with what was known as the "broad arrow slash." This mark meant these trees could be cut only for use by England. The king's pines were those that measured 7 feet in diameter at the butt (or base), stood 225 feet or more in height and yielded 8,300 board feet of timber. The most common use for a king's pine was as a ship's mast, and nearly every coastal Maine town has a "Mast Road" or "Mast Landing" as a result of these early years of harvest. It took tremendous physical labor to hew these massive trees, load them on sledges and haul them from the woods to the coast for shipment to England. As England's plunder of the woodlands continued, colonists began to complain. It can be argued that the Revolutionary War was fought as much over white pine as over tea. The pine came to represent the rich natural resources of America; it was a unique tree, and far too many were being claimed for the king. The broad arrow slash was a red flag to the colonists who were already chafing under England's sovereignty.

The ongoing search for big pines was one of the factors that led to the settlement of Maine. Loggers pushed deeper and deeper into the state as they pursued big timber. Even after the need for king's pines waned, workers stayed to enjoy the rich, wild land that was Maine. Today, white pine still is a major player in Maine's economy, but not to the extent it once was.

At first glance, Maine's woodlands may seem cluttered. Brush, dead trees, fallen logs and layers of leaves are everywhere along the trails. However, every element plays an important role in the forest's ecology; nothing is without purpose.

The brush piles become homes to rabbits, birds and mice; a host of other animals may seek these piles for cover if danger threatens. The many small shrubs of the understory yield nuts and berries, while deer and rabbits browse their tender shoots. Bushes that flower in the warm months attract insects, which in turn are food for birds.

Dead trees and hollow logs provide food and shelter for many species of birds and animals. In the United States, some eighty-nine species of birds and forty-nine mammals commonly use tree cavities, including many Maine species such as chickadees, titmice, wrens, screech owls, great horned owls, wood ducks, woodpeckers, bears, porcupines and raccoons. During the winter, a dozen young gray squirrels might squeeze into one hollow cavity for shelter. Woodpeckers comb the dying trees for insects, and their drilling creates more cavities.

Standing dead timber is important woodland real estate, and often, more than one animal nests in a tree. Look for owl pellets (dry rolls of gray fur) near the base as a sign of an owl home; bits of fur may signal a mammal of some type, while signs of digging could mean a squirrel is nesting here. Squirrels like to stash some food at the base of the tree where they live.

In the spring, the male ruffed grouse drums on a hollow log—his way of attracting a mate. Later, the female grouse finds the log the perfect place to hide her nest and eggs. By late fall, turtles and toads will dig themselves under fallen trees to hibernate for the winter.

When a tree falls, it is not an ending but a beginning. Its death creates an opening in the forest canopy, letting in more light, which encourages seedlings to grow. At the same time, each bit of its skeleton helps ensure the continued health of the forest and its inhabitants.

The forest floor, with its layers of leaves, seeds, nuts, pine spills and pieces of bark, all in various stages of decomposition, is called the "duff." Life bustles beneath these layers of leaves and below them, in the soil, as well. A cubic inch of topsoil contains billions of creatures and is part of a complex food chain that connects all of the forest's residents. Soil-dwelling bacteria and fungi break down dead organic matter into molecules that aboveground plants use for food. When the plants die, the bacteria digest them. Ants and earthworms tunnel through the soil, building passages that allow air and water to enter. Salamanders and moles prowl this underground world, eating insects, while the ovenbird and whip-poor-will nest on the forest floor, knowing an abundant food supply for their young lies in the nearby soil.

Many animals live underground, including chipmunks, woodchucks, foxes, box turtles, salamanders and snakes. Underground dens are warm in winter and cool in summer. As dens are dug, the mixing of the soil helps the forest.

The soil is part of the forest's food chain, as it yields food for the worm, which is food for the bird, which is food for an animal or hawk. Soil-dwelling insects are food for shrews, which are meals for foxes, and so the cycle goes on.

Squirrels hide nuts in the soil, which they may or may not find again. Many of these nuts take root and sprout. These young seedlings become

A gray squirrel looks about for more nuts. *Marcia Peverly photo.*

food for rabbits and deer. Those not browsed will grow and bring renewal to the forest.

Tramping through the woods, it is easy to overlook what lies on the ground. Save for avoiding a wayward branch or rock, most people do not look down. Instead, they seek to spy the bird in the tree or the glimpse of an animal. They do not realize that the duff itself, that cushion of leaves and debris, is key to the health of the forest. The duff acts as fertilizer and provides a protective, insulating layer for the wildflowers that will bloom in spring and for the mushroom and fungi that sprout in fall. The duff insulates the dens of those wintering below and protects the trees' vital roots from erosion. It is as essential a part of the forest as the trees themselves.

An autumn walk almost always yields a scuffle of acorns and other nuts under foot. Nuts are an essential food for wildlife. Every fall, birds and animals prepare for the coming winter by taking advantage of this fall harvest. Oaks, birches, hickories, chestnuts, beeches and walnuts all provide valuable food in the form of nut or "mast" crops. A good mast crop can mean a healthy wildlife population, while a lean year can cause massive squirrel migrations and see a deer herd's fawn population drop by half. Even the success of the black bear's breeding season can be affected. A drop in mast crops also impacts carnivores such as coyotes, bobcats and foxes. If the animals they prey on are less abundant due to less available food, then the predators' food supply is reduced as well.

Mast production can be sporadic from year to year and even from tree to tree. Drought, pollution, insects, disease and tree genetics can all affect the abundance of mast crops. Sometimes trees produce a good yield, but birds and insects gorge themselves on the crop before it hits the ground, thus depriving other species of food.

Acorns are especially important in the late fall and winter when other foods are scarce. They can be the chief food of the ruffed grouse in October and might make up 80 percent of a deer's diet where oaks are abundant. It is interesting to note that gray squirrels store nuts individually, while red squirrels store them in middens, or shallow heaps. These middens may stretch out thirty feet or more. However, neither method is foolproof against thieves—or protection against squirrel forgetfulness.

Many mast crops are popular with humans as well. Acorns are a vital wildlife food, but those from the red and black oaks taste bitter to people due to the presence of tannin. However, Native Americans used acorns from the white oak for flour. They bleached out the tannin with hot water and then pounded the fruit into powder. Roasted and ground, white oak acorns were also brewed as a "wilderness coffee" by the early settlers. Both red and black oaks are common in the Maine woods. Know the red oak by the red striping on its trunk and the black oak by its lack of stripes. Red oak acorns have shallow caps with no fringe and reddish scales. The nut is large and shaped like a barrel. In contrast, the black oak acorn cap is fringed and deep, and the inside is hairy; the nut itself is bowl-shaped. The white oak has light gray, scaly bark and produces an acorn that is oblong with a cap that encloses almost a quarter of the nut. The inside of the cap is hairless.

The American beech is also common in Maine. Beeches are easily spotted by their smooth, gray bark—so tempting to initial carvers—and in autumn, their pale yellow leaves. Two or three beech nuts will be found inside a small, prickly husk. They are tasty both raw and cooked.

Fortunate is the forest with a grove of shagbark hickories. Hickory fruit is very nutritious and a favorite of wildlife. The word "hickory" comes from a Native American name for liquor made from the powdered shells and kernels of the nuts. The Creek Indians pounded hickory nuts into pieces, boiled them and then passed the liquid through five strainers. This preserved the oily part of the liquid, which they called "hickory milk." The milk was sweet, rich and used frequently in their cooking. Shagbarks are easy to identify with their curling bark and large, round, ridged nut husk.

The black walnut is a special find in Maine and extremely valuable for both its wood and its nut crop. Black walnuts are second only to pecans in commercial value. The nut husks can be used to make a brown cloth dye—a common practice of pioneers—but it is the meat inside that is the real prize. Black walnuts like well-drained soils with good sun, preferably near streams. They are often found with red and white oaks, hickories and beech trees. Look for nut husks the size of small, green apples with slight corrugations.

The horse chestnut is familiar to most of us, as its shiny, mahogany-colored nuts quickly draw the eye. Horse chestnuts are not generally eaten by humans, but animals like them. Folklore claims that these nuts can prevent rheumatism, and old-timers may carry a few in their pockets to ward off this ailment. Horse chestnuts are large trees with palmate leaves; look for the nuts inside round, green, prickly husks. They are not native to our woodlands, but so many have been planted around homes and farms that many have "escaped" and might be present in our forests.

Autumn color also paints one of the forest's most delicate plants. Ferns bring a timeless beauty to moist areas, ravines and along the edges of bogs and ponds. They are among the first plants to feel the sting of frost and soon change to autumn colors. Succeeding frosts, and the different reactions of each species, produce an endless variety of colors in these plants, from translucent yellows to deep golds, rich browns, ivories and even faint lime greens. Ferns are primitive plants that first appeared when dinosaurs still roamed the earth. During this time, no flowering plants had yet evolved, and vast forests of giant tree ferns covered a large part of the world. The remains of these ancient plants make up the bulk of today's coal deposits.

There are more than 250 species of ferns in North America; some are no larger than a child's palm, while others stand waist high. Most ferns are perennials, meaning that individual plants come back year after year. Some of these simple, hardy plants have survived more than one hundred years.

Young ferns, which appear in the spring, are called fiddleheads because they resemble the scroll of a violin. The fronds are tightly coiled and covered with protective wool. The fiddleheads of some ferns can be eaten, either simmered like a vegetable or used to flavor salads. They taste like a cross between an avocado and asparagus. Fiddlehead ferns are an old-time Maine dish, and in the springtime, cans of cooked fiddlehead ferns are available in some grocery stores, as well as at specialty food stores.

Some edible species of ferns are bracken, ostrich and cinnamon ferns, but let the experts collect these wild appetizers. The fiddleheads of different species look similar, and some ferns are poisonous.

Over the course of the summer, the tightly coiled fiddleheads unfurl into plumes four and five feet long, depending on the species of fern. Unlike modern plants, ferns reproduce by dust-like particles called spores, rather than through seeds or flowers. Come August, their spore cases split open, releasing millions of spores into the air. Of these, only a few dozen will find sound rooting places and add more ferns to the forest.

Ferns are eaten by many animals, which especially like the bracken fern. Hummingbirds and warblers line their nests with the soft down of the cinnamon fern and the fuzz of uncurling fiddleheads. Ferns are also important soil builders. Their decaying fronds add humus to the soil, making it richer and deeper. Even when not decked with autumn color, ferns add a timeless, primitive beauty to the forest. No other plant has their classic symmetry or flowing patterns. When wind rustles the forest, ferns are waves of gentle motion, and when frost grips the land, freezing the ferns in taut curves, the elegance of their structure is only enhanced.

Exploring Maine's woodlands—save for the vast wilderness of the north—usually yields signs of earlier settlement. Most common are the stone walls, markers of earlier boundaries long forgotten. Some are half-covered by leaves, brush and sediment; others may be crumbling or break off abruptly. All that labor and careful work is now known only to the forest. Elsewhere, the signs may be harder to read—are those giant pines planted in a line? Is that a row of sugar maples? A grove of apple trees might appear, seemingly out of nowhere. These, too, are markers of past lives. The large pines are surveyor's pines, left to indicate a boundary that might later be delineated by a stone wall. Sugar maples were frequently planted near farmhouses for easy syrup harvest in the late winter. Nearly every small farm had an apple orchard, but with the farm long gone, the forest has reclaimed the land. Now, these long-forgotten plantings bring a tremendous boon to wildlife.

These signposts of previous lives are important testaments to the past; they remind us of the determination it took to settle Maine's wild lands and the hopes and dreams of all who came before. The stories of the land's one-time occupants may remain untold, but for a time, the forest remembers that they were here.

"The Week Maine Burned"

Whenever there is an unusually hot and dry fall, many of Maine's older residents become uneasy. They remember the warm October of 1947 and the wildfires that spread across much of the state. Roaring like freight trains, driven on hot winds, the fires consumed more than 200,000 acres of woods, fields and towns. Nine communities were leveled and four severely damaged, and fifteen people lost their lives. Property damage was estimated at $30 million. Livestock, crops, homes, fishing boats, machinery, businesses and all the irreplaceable memorabilia that make up the fabric of people's lives went up in smoke.

The fires consumed the southwestern part of the state, raging from the Lakes Region all the way to the shoreline. Huge sections of Kennebunk, Kennebunkport and Arundel went up in flames. Up on Mount Desert Island, they raced across half the island, burning across the Bubbles, all around Eagle Lake, up over Cadillac Mountain and much of "Millionaire's Row" in picturesque Bar Harbor. They then swept Downeast, where homes in Machias and Jonesport were lost to the conflagration.

The fires seemed unstoppable as they were fed by conditions of extreme drought. Although the spring had been exceedingly wet, the winter had been mild, with a spike of eighty-degree temperatures in March. By June, the rains had stopped. The rest of the summer was hot and sunny, and as August waned, the woods were very dry. September arrived, and still the warmth continued. As the calendar turned toward October, the woods were a tinder box. By October 7, reports of small fires began to come in, and by October 16, there were twenty-four fires burning. Maine was 90 percent forested at the time, so there was plenty of combustible fuel. There was also a shortage of manpower and the kind of sophisticated firefighting technology needed to tackle such a major firestorm. Fire departments were largely volunteer (as they are today), and men were entering the woods with no protective gear, just Indian tanks—hand-operated pumps—strapped to their backs. There were no Hot Shots or Smoke Jumpers, no big tanker trunks and high-capacity hoses, no chemical dumps from aircraft. Townsfolk were literally filling old-fashioned pumper trucks with water brought in in barrels.

In the end, thanks to tremendous bravery and resourcefulness on the part of Maine's people, and with a bit of help in the way of rain from Mother Nature, the fires were put out by the end of the month. But the state of Maine, and those who lived through the fall of '47, were never the same.

Today, the scars of the fires are harder to find. The forests have healed, and towns have rebuilt. But ask an older person about "the great fire" and you need not even say the year. They know. For them, the scars of the fire remain.

Author's note: The great fire came within a few miles of my family's hometown of Eliot. My mother recalls smelling—and tasting—smoke on the air day after day. They had garden hoses lying out around the house in hopes that they could soak it down if the fire came their way. My great-aunt, who had survived fire and earthquake in San Francisco, slept with her clothes on, so terrified was she of being caught unawares. The best book on the subject is *Wildfire Loose: The Week Maine Burned* by Joyce Butler, published by Down East Books.

Chapter 5

The Time of the Hunt

At town halls, town dumps (always a prime advertising spot in rural Maine) and Grange halls and on utility poles, handmade flyers appear: hunters' breakfast this weekend. On Saturday, bright and early, hunters of all ages and descriptions will swarm to the local church hall or firehouse. Dressed in blaze orange and camouflage colors, flannel shirts and wool jackets, ball caps and Bean boots, they chow down on big breakfasts of pancakes and sausage, home fries and beans, muffins and lots of hot coffee. The parking lot is full of pickup trucks, many splashed with mud; gun racks fill the rear windows, and truck beds hold extra gear. Depending on the game, a retriever or pointer might be perched in the front seat, hoping for a treat.

Autumn is the time of the hunt in Maine. The state's abundant wild lands and diverse ecosystems have created a place lush with wildlife, and in the fall, many species are sought with bow and rifle, muzzleloader and shotgun.

Along the Waterways

Although November sees the greatest number of hunters, due to deer-hunting season, the wild harvest begins in September with ducks and geese. As dawn breaks on this crisp October day, a small group of hunters is concealed in the marsh behind a blind. Lying next to them are two Labrador retrievers,

A hunter and his retriever seek game birds in a Maine field. *Courtesy Maine Department of Inland Fisheries & Wildlife.*

among the best duck-hunting dogs in the world. The labs are still, but energy seems to radiate from them. They know what today will bring. The hunters have duck calls, but on this day, they will not be needed.

Gliding among the marsh grasses is a flock of mallards, the males easily spotted with their gleaming emerald heads and ruddy breasts. The females wear feathers of streaky brown; the only flash of color being the blue and white banding on a section of their wings called the speculum. The ducks quack quietly from time to time, and now and then one bobs down under the water, snatching up a bit of aquatic weed. Suddenly, something startles them. As one unit, their wings start to beat; they begin moving across the water at increasing speed, then rise into the air. As they wheel overhead, the white undersides of their wings are dazzling, and the air is alive with the sound of wings. *Bang! Bang, bang!* A rifle barks, and several ducks plummet to earth. Their bodies have barely ruffled the water when the dogs launch into the marsh. Swimming powerfully, they reach their ducks and carry them back to their owners in the gentlest of jaws. Meanwhile, the rest of the flock has swept on, winging out to the bay to regroup and live another day.

Maine's waterways teem with ducks, from the glorious multicolored wood duck of the marshes to bay ducks such as the American pintail, blue-winged teal and black duck. Master divers such as mergansers, buffleheads and goldeneyes paddle the rippling rivers, then plunge deep, catching fish in their sharp bills. Along the ocean's shore, sturdy sea ducks in striking black-and-white plumage ride the swells. This is the domain of scoters, scaups and old squaws, as well as eider ducks down from the far north. Immune to the frigid waters, they come for the abundant fish and will spend the winter here. Their dense plumage and thicker feathers protect them from the cold.

Huge flocks of Canada geese soar in by the tens of thousands, down from the Hudson's Bay area and beyond. They will winter over in the northern United States, swarming every bay and visiting farmers' fields to scavenge leftover corn and grain. Known by the striking white cheek patch on their ebony heads, they are so abundant that it is not uncommon to see hundreds at one time.

Birds Afield

As the fall meadows turn to gold and foliage color begins to peak, hunters take to the meadows and woodlands in search of game birds. They seek the funny little woodcock with its long beak, the ruffled grouse (known as partridge in Maine), the ring-necked pheasant, the snipe and rails. Pheasants are not native to North America, having been brought over from Asia centuries ago, but they have adapted well to their adopted country and are now found throughout its northern tier. Some hunters work the fields with dogs, creating a symmetry of silent communication as the dog ranges quietly ahead, then goes on point indicating a bird is near. After the bird is flushed and shot, the dog will be signaled to retrieve the bird.

The woodcock is a curious-looking bird with a short, stubby body and a long, pointed bill. It feeds extensively on worms, and you can often tell woodcock habitat by the borings he makes in the soft soil of woodlands and old fields as he searches for food. In the twilight of a spring night, the male performs an elaborate courtship dance, making his sharp "peent" call while on the ground and then spiraling upward slowly to a great height; he then descends in a series of zigzags so rapidly that the rushing wind causes his wings to make a whistling sound. He returns to the same spot and repeats his dance, which hopefully impresses any nearby females. The female woodcock has tricks of her own; she is known for deploying the tactic of a pretended broken wing to lure would-be prey from her nested young.

Among the most prized game bird is the ruffed grouse, a chicken-like bird that relies on aspen groves for food and shelter. Their plumage, with its shades of gold, brown and bands of black, allows them to easily blend in with leaves and brush. When flushed, they explode from cover with a great flapping of wings, designed to discombobulate their prey. They rocket straight up in the air, tail feathers fanned out, then swiftly turn and soar off to another concealed spot—usually nearby. (Grouse can fly quietly if they wish, but the explosion tactic works well in throwing off an attack and, by its noise, confuses predators about just how many birds were flushed.)

Because of their swift and agile flying, grouses can be among the more challenging birds to hunt. However, this was not always the case. In the early days of this country, grouse were incredibly abundant and evidently somewhat mystified by the early settlers. They did not immediately perceive them as a threat; it was not unusual for a person to encounter a grouse calmly going about its business in the forest, completely unperturbed by a human nearby. Colonists tell of easily getting close to the birds and then taking them out with a well-placed rock. As grouse hunting increased, the birds finally realized the human danger and adapted by becoming the wily targets they are today.

Perhaps no game bird is more striking then the male ring-necked pheasant with its iridescent plumage, bronze breast, green and purple head, long tail feathers of banded gold and striking white neck ring. Pheasants are among the most popular game birds in the world and were hunted for centuries in Europe and Asia before being successfully introduced here in the 1880s. Once a viable wild population was thriving, the bird steadily spread its range across much of the United States. Ring-necked pheasants are also similar to chickens and are commonly found in grasslands and on the edges of agricultural areas. They are known for their tasty flesh, and their tail feathers were once sought for decorating ladies' millinery.

TALKING TURKEY

October is also the time for hunting wild turkeys, large, dark birds that may be sighted in flocks of forty or more throughout the state. They are typically seen in woodlands and along the edge of meadows, and it is not unusual to

A wild turkey searches for food in a Maine woodland. *Marcia Peverly photo.*

see them foraging in broad daylight. Wild turkeys are omnivorous, feeding on acorns, nuts, seeds, berries, roots, insects and even small amphibians and snakes. They are cautious birds and will run or fly at the first sign of danger. Despite their large size, they are expert flyers (unlike their plump domestic cousins) and able to weave through trees at high speed until they feel it is safe to roost.

The North American wild turkey (*Meleagris gallopavo*) bears little resemblance to the plump butterball we typically enjoy, even though they are the same species. Our domestic bird was domesticated from a South Mexican subspecies of wild turkey and is bred to have a big chest and sturdy thighs—basically, more meat.

While the domestic turkey is virtually flightless, the wild turkey is a fearless flyer, capable of zipping through woodlands for a mile or more. Male turkeys, called toms (females are hens), are amazingly colorful, with reddish-yellow legs, red throats and wattles, dark bodies, bronze wings and iridescent feathers with areas of red, purple, green, copper, bronze and gold. As a finishing touch, a tuft of coarse hair called a beard typically adorns their chests. Their heads can be red or blue, depending on their mood. When males are excited, their heads turn blue; when ready to fight, they turn red.

A flock of wild turkeys makes its way through a Maine woodland. *Marcia Peverly photo.*

According to the National Turkey Association, the largest recorded adult turkey weighed in at a whopping thirty-eight pounds, but most adult males weigh only eleven to twenty-four pounds. The smaller females run five to twelve pounds.

Wild turkeys are good eating and have been zealously hunted since colonial times—so much so that by the 1940s their numbers were down to only about thirty thousand nationwide. U.S. Fish and Game officials made a tremendous effort to reinstate the bird, and turkey numbers rebounded dramatically. Today, more than seven million birds roam in large flocks throughout the country. The eastern wild turkey subspecies is the most abundant and once again a popular game bird.

One wildlife biologist reports that he notices "no real difference" between the meat of the domestic turkey and that of the wild bird. "The leg meat can be tougher, but the breast meat is tender and to me tastes like veal cutlets if sliced just right. Basically, you may just need to cook the legs a bit longer. I also have used the legs, neck and wings in a stew, and it was very good."

Turkey was part of the Pilgrims' original feast (along with waterfowl, venison, fish, lobster, clams, berries, pumpkins and squash), but it did not become the official Thanksgiving Day dinner until around 1857. Nonetheless, there were many early fans of the bird. The idea that Benjamin Franklin sought the turkey as the national bird of the United States comes from a letter he wrote to his daughter Sarah Bache on January 26, 1784. In this, he criticized the choice of the bald eagle as the national bird and suggested that a turkey would be a better choice. He is quoted as saying:

> *I am on this account not displeased that the Figure is not known as a Bald Eagle, but looks more like a Turkey. For in truth, the Turkey is in Comparison a much more respectable Bird, and withal a true original Native of America...He is besides, though a little vain & silly, a Bird of Courage, and would not hesitate to attack a Grenadier of the British Guards who should presume to invade his Farm Yard with a red Coat on.*

Brave, colorful, tasty—what more could one want in a national bird!

BIGGER GAME

Abundant Black Bears

Lumbering through the Maine woods is the state's largest carnivore, a handsome bear with a glossy black coat and white bib. Fall is a good time to see one, as the bears are engaged in last-minute feeding before their winter sleep. As bears go, *Ursus americanus* is relatively mild-mannered and not known for demonstrating the sometimes more aggressive behavior of the American grizzly or Alaskan brown bear. Still, anyone should be wary of a wild animal standing up to six feet tall, weighing in at around 350 pounds (males) and able to run at speeds of up to thirty-five miles per hour. Black bear attacks are rare but have occurred.

Native Americans had enormous respect for black bears, seeing them as epitomizing strength and courage and providing healing spirits. When they hunted bears, they asked permission of the spirit gods for the kill and offered prayers of both apology and thanks afterward, thus honoring the spirit of the bear and its sacrifice.

After Minnesota, Maine has the second-largest population of black bears in the country, with more than twenty-three thousand within its borders. However, this number fluctuates, and some years there has been concern

A black bear forages. Bears will stuff themselves twenty-four hours a day from August through October as they prepare for hibernation. *Photo courtesy Mark Latti, Maine Wildlife Park.*

about population dips. Part of the concern stems from the fact that the reproductive rate of black bears tends to be low. About two to three cubs are born per litter, but black bears do not mate until the females are between three and five years old and the males four to six years old. Once the cubs are born, the odds that they will make it to maturity are not ideal. Cub mortality is about 20 percent, with yearling mortality at about 35 percent. Newborn bears are about the size of a chipmunk; they are toothless, blind, deaf and only lightly furred. The mother will nurse them in her den for about three months. As they grow and are able to venture farther afield, the sow (as females are called) finds "safety trees" for them. These are usually white pines or hemlocks with deeply furrowed bark and large branches that the cubs can easily run up. The mother will leave them there to sleep while she forages nearby. Both infant bears and cubs are vulnerable to predation by eagles, coyotes, other adult bears and, where present, cougars and wolves. Their very protective mother will keep them in her care for about two years.

In areas where black bears are hunted, their average lifespan is about three to five years; those not taken by hunters can live twenty years. Thus, it is a delicate balance to ensure that enough bears survive the hunt to maintain a sustainable breeding population. In Maine, careful monitoring has helped ensure good numbers of bears, and a big game license allows for only one bear per season.

Despite the black bear's significant size, anywhere from 75 to 90 percent of its diet is vegetarian. Black bears are true "gourmets," enjoying a wide and diverse diet that encompasses berries, currants, acorns, nuts, cherries, grass, roots, leaves, buds, the inner bark of coniferous trees, ants, grubs, caterpillars, fish, frogs, eggs, birds, small mammals, fawns, moose calves and carrion. Just like Winnie the Pooh, black bears enjoy honey and will dig out wild honey deposits in old tree snags. Like Yogi, they will also scavenge picnic areas and campgrounds. They consider bird feeders another wonderful find, and many Mainers have seen their feeders dragged away by a hungry bruin or that other scalawag, the raccoon.

A black bear's diet changes as the seasons pass from spring to fall, with the bear indulging in ever more high-calorie food as late autumn, and hibernation, approach. From August to October, bears will literally stuff themselves twenty-four hours a day, devouring high-fat and high-protein acorns, beechnuts, hazelnuts, mountain ash berries, cherries and any other available late berries. Before entering their long winter's sleep, the bears fast for a week and then forage once more, this time eating dry leaves, grass, pine needles and hair. These items form a wad that effectively seals their other end for the next six months or so. While sleeping, a bear will live off its stored body fat without losing muscle; he will not urinate or pass waste. The urine from his bladder is recycled by his kidneys into new protein, and water from the recycled urine will prevent dehydration. He will awaken sometime in mid-April to early May, groggy but otherwise in good health.

The black bear is not the state animal of Maine—that honor goes to the moose—but it is the emblem of the University of Maine sports teams. Bananas the Black Bear has fiercely urged his charges on to top rankings in hockey, football and baseball. From 1914 until 1966, a real black bear named Bananas attended U-Maine games and rallies. It all started when a black bear cub, found on Mount Katahdin, was given to the Old Town chief of police by an Old Town Native American guide. The cub was named Jeff, and the police chief loaned him to the U-Maine football team in hopes that he might motivate it to victory. Jeff was introduced at a football rally, and when the tiny bear entered the auditorium, the crowd roared. The surprised bear then stood on his head, and the crowd went "bananas." That season, the university football team overwhelmed its opponents, and from then on, it was called the U-Maine Black Bears.

From 1914 to 1966, a live black bear was the mascot of the University of Maine sports teams. The first little cub was called Bananas, and so each succeeding bear kept the name. Today, U-Maine has a person in a bear costume act as the mascot, but the name Bananas remains. Here, Bananas IV and George Stackpole, class of 1924, ride to the Bowdoin College game in a 1918 Model T Ford Phaeton owned by Cyril G. Cogswell, class of 1927. *Photo courtesy of Fogler Library Special Collections, University of Maine.*

Over the next several decades, various bears named Bananas became university mascots. Each one lived in a den by the Stillwater River and was cared for by the brothers of Beta Theta Pi. Bananas II and III took to fraternity life, riding the trolley with their brethren into town, where they indulged in a few beers—either in celebration or to drown their sorrows, depending on how Maine's teams fared. Bananas III developed quite a taste for beer and was said to have actually suffered a hangover after one particularly rowdy episode. Bananas IV spent the summer at the Atlantis Hotel on Kennebunk Beach, rollicking in the sand and befriending a local dog named Jiggs. When summer ended and Bananas left, the dog so missed his friend that he began to pine. Jiggs's owner gave up and sent the dog to live in Orono with his bear companion. The use of live bears as mascots ended in 1966, and today, a human in a Bananas costume rallies the sports teams to victory.

The Moose Mystique

According to the Micmac, a Native American tribe whose range once spanned southeastern Canada, the Maritime Provinces and northern Maine, the Ninth Moon of September is the Moose-Calling Moon. Micmac lore goes like this:

> *In the season when leaves begin to turn color, we go down to the lakes and, with birch-bark horns, make that sound which echoes through the spruce trees, the call of a moose looking for a mate: Mooo-ahhh-ahhh, Mooo-ahhh-ahhh. If we wait there, patient in our canoes, the Moose will come. His great horns are flat because, long ago, before people came, Gloos-kap asked the Moose what he would do when he saw human beings. "I will throw them up high on my sharp horns," Moose said. So Gloos-kap pushed his horns flatter and made him smaller. "Now, Moose," he said, "you will not want to harm my people." So the Moose comes and stands, strong as the northeast wind. He looks at us, then we watch him disappear back into the willows again.*

Seeing a moose (*Alces alces*) is an incredible experience. Their coats are reddish brown to nearly black with grayish white lower legs and brown calves. Moose are the largest animal in the Northeast, with males standing five to seven feet high at the shoulders. A bull can weigh 880 to 1,190 pounds, while cows are a "dainty" 825 to 1,170. Add to that the fact that males are about seven to ten feet long and may be crowned with an antler rack spreading up to five feet and you have one impressive animal.

Yet for all their great size, there is something about the moose that is kind of goofy and endearing. Is it the scraggly little beard on their chins? The cow-like muzzle and big floppy ears? Or the fact that most of the time, moose usually stand calmly at the edge of lakes and ponds, munching on water lilies (a favorite food), even when canoeists paddle close by? Unlike their cousins the deer, which bolt at the slightest whisper of something amiss, moose often seem to be in a Zen-like state, focusing primarily on eating and relaxing as opposed to burning up needed energy by taking flight. It is easy to see why food is a priority, as moose eat about fifty-five to sixty-five pounds per day in summer and thirty-three to forty-five pounds in winter, with chosen foods being salt-rich aquatic plants in summer and twigs and bark (once the sap starts to run) in winter. In fact, the name moose comes from the Algonquian word *moosee*, meaning "bark or twig eater."

While moose are normally placid, a cow with a calf is best let be; nor are moose to be disturbed during the rut. The fall rut peaks in late September and early October, and during this time, lovesick males become unpredictable and aggressive. The bulls' moods start to change in late August. By this time, their antlers have been growing for five months and are covered with velvet—a soft, blood vessel–rich covering that nourishes the antlers as they grow. Now, the moose begin rubbing off the velvet on tree branches and trunks. With the velvet gone, the bulls' huge racks are stained orange brown with dried blood. Males now start challenging one another in order to establish breeding status. These challenges are literally a contest of who has the biggest rack, with the less impressive of two contesting bulls usually backing down before any physical combat ensues. Occasionally, though, moose do butt heads, and the crack of antlers crashing together resounds throughout the forest. Because female moose are impressed by big antlers (sad to say, in the moose world size *does* matter), young bulls rarely get to mate. In fact, cows are very vocal about seeking a bull. They will low constantly for forty hours to attract a mate, making the woods one noisy place during the rut.

In some cases, lovelorn moose act downright crazy when it comes to choosing a mate. Rutting moose have appeared confused about who their competitors are, often challenging bizarre objects to duels. Bulls have chased humans up trees, charged and demolished trucks in head-on collisions and even taken on trains. Some moose have mistaken cattle and horses for potential mates. Most well known is the 1986 case of a Vermont moose that, for seventy-six days, wooed and occasionally nuzzled a brown-and-white Hereford cow named Jessica. Once his antlers dropped in December, the spell was broken, and the would-be suitor slunk off into the woods. A few years ago, a similarly lovesick moose mooned after a horse for several weeks.

Cows are very protective of their offspring and are dangerous if their calves are threatened or approached. Moms usually keep their offspring isolated for as long as possible, hiding them on islands, in swamps or in alder thickets to avoid predators, such as bears. Calves are born in May and June, with usually just one per birth. A baby moose is about three feet long and may weigh between twenty-five and thirty-five pounds. Their mother's rich milk allows them to grow faster than any other North American mammal—gaining more than two pounds per day their first month and up to seven pounds a day afterward.

Moose love to swim and take to the water frequently to feed and to avoid the hordes of black flies so common in Maine. Sometimes, if the calf has tired, it will seek out its mother and rest its head or front legs over its mother's neck as she swims. Moose are not only strong swimmers, but they are also competent divers, with dives of up to twenty feet having been recorded. The maximum time under water is fifty seconds.

After a year, young moose are pushed away to set out on their own. Some wander far as they search for their own territories or mates. A yearling named Alice was tagged in the Adirondacks in 1998 and then turned up in Ontario's Algonquin Park some two hundred miles away three years later.

Moose are found all over Maine, but the highest concentration is in the Lakes Region and Great North Woods. They like forests of broad-leaf trees mixed with mature conifers, with wetlands—lakes, beaver ponds, swamps—and meadows nearby. On average, a moose in the wild will live seven or eight years, but ancients as old as nineteen years have been recorded.

Maine's deep winter snows can be hard on the deer herd, but the long-legged moose handles winters fairly easily. Ironically, the biggest threats to moose are a tiny worm and a tiny tick. The brain worm parasite is spread by white-tailed deer, although the deer are themselves not victims. More than a century ago, logging opened up the Great North Woods, and as new growth sprouted in the cut-over areas, the deer population boomed, along with the brain worm. The moose population plummeted as the disease spread, and the situation became so dire that moose hunting was banned from 1935 to 1980. Then, as logging waned and forests matured again, the deer population dropped, the parasite receded and moose numbers rebounded.

Winter ticks, which were first documented in the 1930s, also can take a toll on the moose population. Calves going through their first winter are especially vulnerable as their smaller body size makes it harder for them to withstand a tick infestation. Tick populations wax and wane, as does their impact on the moose herd.

Today, there are estimated to be 29,000 moose in Maine. About 2,600 are harvested each year. The Maine Department of Inland Fisheries & Wildlife sets permit limits each year based on population in order to ensure that healthy numbers of moose endure.

Maine's highest mountain, and the third highest in New England, is Katahdin, located in Baxter State Park. Rising 5,269 feet, *Katahdin* means "Greatest Mountain" in the language of the Penobscot. To them, Katahdin's knife-edged peak was home to Pamola, the storm god, a fierce spirit with the head of a moose, the wings of an eagle and the body of a man. For this reason, many Native Americans gave Katahdin's summit area a wide birth. Although this moose spirit had at times a terrifying aspect, the moose itself was highly valued by Native Americans. A single animal could feed an entire family through the winter; its hide also yielded leather for moccasins, and the wool from its mane or beard was used for mittens and socks.

Today, moose taken in the hunt are equally important to many Maine families. Maine can be a harsh place to make a living, as many traditional industries have closed. The great cotton mills, shoe factories, logging industries and canneries are gone or reduced in scope. The vast wild lands that give Maine its beauty and abundance of natural resources also mean that urban centers and jobs are scarce. For this reason, many Mainers hunt and fish not just for sport but also to supplement their food stores. A moose means just as much today as it did centuries ago.

Moose also provide an unexpected, and somewhat humorous, product. In summer, their scat or droppings are squishy brown "cow pies." But in winter, when their diet is more twig and bark based, the scat changes to greenish-tinged or dark brown fiber pellets about the size of an olive or pecan. These dried pellets have become popular as a spruce-scented incense and are also varnished and sold as jewelry. A unique way for memories of Maine's moose to live on!

White-Tailed Deer: The Woodland "Ghost"

The November sun is barely a scarlet rim on the horizon when one sees the first pickup trucks along the side of the road; a few more are pulled up under the high transmission lines, where they cut a wide swath through the woods. Deep in the forest or crouched in the brush, men—and some women—are hoping for that first sight of Maine's number one big game animal: the white-tailed deer (*Odocoileus virginianus*).

Hunting a white-tailed deer can be like hunting a ghost with superhero powers. Their brown coats and capacity for standing utterly still allow them to easily blend in with woodland thickets and fall foliage. Add to that the fact that deer are always on alert, and you have a formidable quarry. Their eyes are constantly roving from side to side, checking their surroundings. Their huge ears continuously twitch forward and back, like mini radars capable of picking up the slightest sound. Their sense of smell is also sharp, and they seem to filter every molecule of air in their surroundings. A buck will stamp and snort because he can smell a person but cannot yet locate him. The snorting and stomping is his ploy to make the human move so he can pinpoint where the threat lies.

When a deer is spooked, it demonstrates the extraordinary athleticism that makes it such prized prey. White-tails can leap up to twenty feet in a single bound and can easily clear heights of seven to nine feet. Their movement is explosive—a few quick bounds, and they are out of the open and deep into the woods, their presence just a memory. As they flee, they raise their tails, flashing a white flag that alerts other deer to danger.

In the wild, the greatest danger to white-tailed deer are predators such as coyotes, bears, cougars and wolves (where present), although fawns can be taken by smaller hunters such as bobcats, foxes and lynx. Winter takes the greatest toll on a herd, with 15 to 20 percent of deer starving in the deep snows. If the winter is mild, the deer population can boom come springtime.

A doe gives birth to anywhere from one to three fawns in May and June, with some births taking place later in the summer. The delicate fawns weigh three and a half to eight pounds, and their coats are covered with white spots. They have no scent, and their speckled fur provides the perfect camouflage as they nest in the long grass or deep forest groves. The mother teaches them to lie perfectly still while she slips off to feed, letting their disguise and lack of scent be their protection. Even so, fawn mortality runs anywhere from 20 to 40 percent. (In high agricultural areas, fawns can also fall victim to mowing machines.)

Like moose, deer rut in the fall, and by November, bucks are parading around with full racks and swelling necks, strutting their prowess and jostling for territory and mates. They will butt heads with rivals, and as with moose, the larger, older bucks tend to win breeding rights. Deer are in their prime at between four and six years of age, and a full-grown buck may weigh two to three hundred pounds. Deer drop their antlers as winter nears, and with them goes their aggression. Native Americans prized deer antlers and often used them to decorate headdresses; they believed that wearing antlers made one supersensitive to his surroundings. The fallen antlers are a boon to other forest creatures, being a rich source of calcium and salt for chipmunks, mice, porcupines and rabbits.

About 330,000 white-tailed deer live in Maine. They feed primarily on plants, wild flowers, seedlings, saplings, moss, lichens and mast crops. Near suburban areas, they can wreak havoc on gardens. In winter, they will heavily browse twigs and bark, and if conditions are harsh, it is not unusual to see bark stripped off trees at the six-foot mark as desperate deer stand on their hind legs to reach food.

THE HUNTERS

Most people dream of winning the lottery, but in Maine, that lottery might not be for cash but for moose. Cyrus Morgan of North Berwick saw his dream of hunting moose come true when he won the lottery for a hunting permit in 2010. Cyrus had been playing the lottery for ten years and wondered if his number would ever come up. As he entered his ticket at Cabella's, he was hopeful but not confident, so he was shocked when his phone rang and a friend who worked at the store said Cyrus's name had been called.

"I was ecstatic!" he recalls. "I've been hunting all my life, mostly white-tailed deer, and two of my dreams were to hunt elk out West and to hunt moose here in Maine. Finally, one of them had come true."

Hunters can apply to enter the moose permit lottery in April; once their applications are approved, they have to wait until the winners are drawn in June. The lottery is run by Maine's Department of Inland Fisheries and Wildlife and is open to both residents and nonresidents. The moose lottery allows a certain number of names to be drawn each year, based on the sustainability of the moose population. About three thousand permits are issued in any given year. Each hunter is assigned a zone to hunt within and is given five days to bag a moose. As of 2011, if a hunter is not successful, he must wait three years before he can be allotted another permit.

Cyrus had primarily hunted in the woods around his home and in the North New Portland area. The zone he was assigned was in Jackman, a rugged wilderness area along Route 201 and the site of Benedict Arnold's desperate march to Quebec.

"We got up there on a Saturday night and started hunting on Sunday," he recalls. "We saw signs and kept tracking Monday, Tuesday and Wednesday. At first, I was only seeing cows and calves, no bulls, which was all my permit allowed me to hunt. Finally, on Thursday, I got my moose." (Three types of permits are issued: for bulls only, for antlerless moose (young bulls or cows) and for bulls or cows.)

Cyrus's kill was estimated to be about two years old, a young bull with a thirty-inch rack. Moose (and other game animals) must be taken to Inland Fisheries and Wildlife's weigh stations to have their stats recorded. Wardens estimate the age of the animals by taking one of their teeth. Hunters get a copy of the report and can also look up information about their kills online.

Guides tell of hunters who become so excited that they can barely fire their weapons when they sight their first moose, but Cyrus had no problem. "When I had the bull in my sights, my reaction was automatic," he says. "All

Mainers prepare to enjoy the spoils of a fall hunt. *Photo by George French, courtesy of the Maine State Archives.*

those years of hunting kicked in, and the minute I had the gun up on my shoulder, I just drew a bead and fired."

Cyrus had heard stories of novice moose hunters who bagged their prize and then had no idea how to get such an enormous animal out of the woods. He planned ahead, bringing chain saws for clearing a path and a block and tackle, and he had a butcher lined up nearby.

"My moose weighed 575 pounds, and 300 pounds of that was meat," he says. "Three years later, we still have some. It is the best red meat I have ever had. It's not like venison; it's lean but very flavorful. I gave a lot to family and friends, and everyone loves it."

While bagging game is the main goal of hunting, most hunters will tell you that the hunt is about more than that. For true sportsmen, it is a time of being part of something bigger. They speak of the hold that the wild country has on them, of knowing how insignificant you are in the presence of such vastness. They respect the animals they hunt, and most also work diligently to ensure that the habitat that sustains these animals is protected. Hunting is a love affair—not just with the hunt but also with the land and all it provides.

For veteran sportsman Paul Fuller, hunting in Maine is a life-long passion. Paul ran the popular Eastern Fishing & Outdoor Exhibition series of sport shows for years and is still a consultant with the organization; he continues to write a regular outdoor column and hosts a cable television show on hunting and bird dog training (*Bird Dogs Afield TV*). He has been hunting in Maine since the 1970s, covering much of the state on various excursions for everything from deer to bear and game birds. While he deems all of the state spectacular, his favorite hunting spot is the North Maine Woods. "It's remote and beautiful, and frequently you can go there and never see another person the entire time you are there," he says. "I also love the Rangeley Lakes area. In the fall, this is one of the most beautiful places in Maine. I've hiked up many a trail in the western mountains. To see this panorama of Maine and New Hampshire spread before you, with gorgeous fall color at its height—it is awe-inspiring. I have hunted and fished all over the United States and seen many lovely places, but none are as beautiful as Maine in fall. Part of that beauty is fleeting, as peak foliage is only a few weeks and it is gone, but that only makes the fall all the more special."

Today, Paul primarily hunts ruffed grouse, woodcock and turkey, usually hunting over a bird dog. He loves the camaraderie of Maine's deep woods sporting camps and the remote little towns of the wilderness. "Maine is unique," he says. "The little towns along the Allagash are like the frontier towns of a century ago. Time seems to have stopped here. Just north of Rockwood on Moosehead Lake, there is an old farm that you see as you enter the North Maine Woods; it's been there for one hundred years and always looks the same. It's part of the landscape."

Paul remembers driving to Quebec in 1972 and seeing a logging drive on Maine's Kennebec River. He stopped to watch. It turned out to be one of the last log drives, as the practice was stopped in 1976. He was also one of the first people to whitewater raft in Maine. Wayne Hockmeyer started the first whitewater rafting venture on the Kennebec out of Rockwood in 1978. He had taken just two trips down the river when he invited Paul and some friends to go with him. "I remember we hurtled through the Three Sisters and flipped twice," says Paul. "As we continued on, Wayne said, 'Look around. Only about one hundred people have ever seen this scenery.' Before he started doing the trips, the river was so wild and the region so remote that few people ever went down the river. It was true wilderness."

Each year, Paul has at least one episode of his television show film in Maine. "Hunting in Maine is always popular with viewers," he says. "The natural resources here are amazing. There is always something beautiful or exciting to film. The vastness itself casts a spell. You could spend multiple lifetimes here and never explore all of Maine."

Maine hunters come in all shapes and sizes, but one of the best is a young woman from North Berwick. At age seventeen, Amy Royal completed hunting's "Grand Slam" by bagging a moose, bear, deer and turkey all in one season. Called "Annie Oakley" by her friends, Amy has spent time in the woods since she was a baby riding in her father's backpack on woodland hikes. Hunting is in her blood, as the entire family hunts, including her mother and sister. Amy started hunting at age ten, taught by her dad. She first tried for the slam at age fifteen but missed her bear.

The year 2006 turned out to be Amy's time. She shot her turkey first and then took down a moose on September 26. She bagged her bear four days later and then got her deer. Her turkey was a beautiful gobbler; the bear, which was taken up on Mahoosuc Mountain, was 260 pounds; the moose, shot in Zone 4 (the North Maine Woods), tipped the scales at 666, and the deer was 70 pounds. Amy is no stranger to taking big game—a moose taken in an earlier season weighed in at 1,094 pounds. (Prior to 2011, residents could enter the moose lottery more frequently; there was no three-year wait.)

Throughout her high school years, Amy was a solid student and competitive gymnast who got up at 3:30 a.m. to hunt during the season. After graduation, she planned to attend Maine Guide School in hopes of soon sharing her expertise with other hunters.

THE GUIDES

Maine has a long history of outdoor guides. The state's heavily forested interior and rugged coastline have encouraged outdoor pursuits such as fishing, hunting, canoeing, sea kayaking and, along with them, the need for expert guides. In Maine, a "guide" is anyone who accepts a fee for services in "accompanying or assisting anyone in the field, forest, waters or ice… while hunting, fishing, trapping, boating, snowmobiling, or camping at a primitive camping area," according to the Maine Department of Inland Fisheries & Wildlife.

The first Maine Guide was licensed in 1897 and was a woman called "Fly Rod Crosby." That first year, 1,700 guides were licensed. At the time, guiding was primarily for hunters and fishermen. Big game hunting (deer and bear) was the mainstay of a guide's income, with fishing on inland lakes and streams a close second. Canoe trips were also starting to gain in popularity.

For many years, Maine Guides were not required to pass any standardized test. Interested parties simply were reviewed by the local game warden, and if they passed muster with him, they were considered fit to be guides. (This was not as lax as it might seem, as most folks in rural communities knew one another, and most wardens had a pretty good idea of who was fit and who was not.)

As the number of guide applicants continued to grow, it became necessary to create a standardized test, and in 1975, the current system was launched. It requires a written and oral examination pertinent to the guide's stated area of expertise, such as sea kayaking, hunting, fishing, whitewater rafting or recreation. (Certification is given only in these areas, and for white-water rafting, the guides are registered for specific rivers.) The tests also require the guide to have expertise in navigation (map and compass on land), first aid, motorboat operation, survival skills and rescue skills, among others. Most guides specialize in one area, but some guides have experience in several areas and become certified as master guides.

There are currently four thousand registered Maine Guides, and most are independent small businesses. They may work alone or contract with sporting camps or other businesses. The Maine Professional Guides Association is composed of registered Maine Guides who are working to improve the criteria and ethics of a growing industry. However, not all registered Maine Guides are members of the Maine Professional Guides Association.

To search for a registered Maine Guide by town, company or area of expertise, visit www.maineguides.org. Local town halls, sporting goods stores, sporting camps and other outdoor venues often have this information as well.

Maine's brilliant fall leaves cast colorful patterns on the ground. *Marcia Peverly photo.*

An overcast sky is a dramatic backdrop to autumn color. *Marcia Peverly photo.*

Colorful foliage rims a Maine pond. *Marcia Peverly photo.*

Autumn color is just starting to show on this hillside. *Marcia Peverly photo.*

Autumn flowers mingle with colorful leaves. *Marcia Peverly photo.*

A tranquil day at a Maine lake. *Marcia Peverly photo.*

Left: A typical woodland pond aglow with fall color. *Marcia Peverly photo.*

Below: The historic Fryeburg Fair draws a huge crowd each fall. *Marcia Peverly photo.*

Giant pumpkin carving is one of the highlights of the Damariscotta Pumpkinfest. *Dr. Diane H. Ranes PhD photo.*

A mallard drake glides amid fall leaves. *Marcia Peverly photo.*

A mallard pair patrols a Maine pond. *Marcia Peverly photo.*

Right: One of Maine's big black bears ambles through a field. *Photo Mark Latti, Maine Wildlife Park.*

Below: A hunter and his bird dog look for game birds. *Photo courtesy Maine Department of Inland Fisheries & Wildlife.*

Above: Maine's apples ripe for picking. Apples are the taste of fall. *Marcia Peverly photo.*

Left: Fall is the perfect time for enjoying a glass of cider on the porch. *Photo Budd Perry, Memories Studio.*

Opposite, top: A contestant in the Damariscotta Pumpkinfest Regatta paddles her giant pumpkin boat. *Ronn Orenstein Photography.*

Opposite, bottom: Warm apple cider doughnuts are a classic taste of fall. *Photo courtesy of* The Cooking of Joy.

Doughnuts paired with cider are an ideal combination. *Photo courtesy of flickr photographer regan76.*

Apples are one of Maine's classic fall crops; the state has more than eighty-four orchards covering two thousand acres. *Photo courtesy of flickr photographer net_efekt.*

Top: The Bass Harbor Lighthouse glows in the fading light of an autumn day. *Photo courtesy of flickr photographer Chris Potako.*

Middle: Maine's forests put on a brilliant color show in the fall. *Photo courtesy of flickr photographer Werner Kunz.*

Right: The ruffed grouse, or partridge, as it is called in Maine, is one of the state's most popular game birds. *Photo courtesy of flickr photographer Seabamirum.*

Close-up of a red-tailed hawk. Mount Agamenticus in York, Maine, is an excellent spot for viewing the fall raptor migration. *Photo courtesy of state park staff.*

A view of Portland Headlight, Maine's most photographed lighthouse, which was commissioned in 1792 by President George Washington. *Photo couresy of flickr photographer jodycl.*

Above: Maine has a thriving moose population. Note this bull's massive rack (antlers). Moose antlers can reach widths of six feet or more. *Photo courtesy Lisa Kane, Maine Wildlife Park.*

Right: Homemade apple pie is a true slice of autumn. *Photo by Budd Perry, Memories Studio.*

A "piggy portrait" at the fair. *Photo courtesy of flickr photographer bertconcepts.*

Pumpkins are a popular fall crop, both for pies and for decorating.

A sheep strikes a pose.

Gray squirrels are in abundance in Maine; in autumn, they stockpile vast amounts of nuts as food for the coming winter. *Photo courtesy of flickr photographer likeaduck.*

A male, or tom, turkey struts his stuff. Wild turkeys are abundant in Maine, creating excellent hunting opportunities. *Photo courtesy of Steve Voght.*

Kayakers paddle down the foliage-lined Presumpscot River beneath Babb's Bridge. *Photo by Vicki Lund.*

How to Get the Most from a Nature Walk

People sometimes wonder why they do not see more animals when they go on nature walks, but wildlife is all around. Looking for clues, and adopting a change of approach, can greatly improve wildlife sightings.

* **Choose the right time of day**. Most birds and animals are more active in the early morning and early evening then at midday.
* **Be quiet**. Animals have keen hearing and can detect a person's approach long before the animal is seen. All animals have enemies, and since humans are bigger than most animals, it is not surprising that they hide when they hear people coming. Stay quiet; stop, wait and listen. This increases your chances of seeing animals. Chattering and moving about will scare them away.
* **Listen**. Birds are heard before they are seen. Every bird species has its own distinctive song. Birds sing most in the early morning and late afternoon and evening.
* **Look for clues on thorny thickets and barbed-wire fences**. One might find the hairs of foxes, deer or rabbits caught there. Feathers are easy to find. Finding feathers or hair often in the same place is a clue that there may be a den or nest nearby or that a game trail runs through here.
* **Check for nests and holes**. The burrows of chipmunks and foxes are easy to see. The size of the burrow will give you a clue about what made it. Look for signs that it is still occupied—are there food remains, droppings or hairs? You might find some well-worn tracks leading away from the burrow. Some animals follow the same paths when they go out hunting for food.
* **Bird nests are easy to find**. Note the size of the nest and what it is made of inside and outside. Are there any features to give you clues?
* **Animals are untidy eaters**. Many leave the remains of their food on the ground. Different animals feed in different ways. Squirrels split nutshells in half, while voles gnaw a round hole through them. Dormice and voles leave a smooth edge to the hole, while wood mice leave teeth marks. Nuthatches and woodpeckers often wedge nuts in tree bark, either as a storage place or to hold nuts firm while they hammer them open.

* **Look on the ground**. Tracks are more easily found when the ground is soft or covered with snow. Good places to look are in the mud beside streams and ponds, in sandy areas and in areas where the soil is not covered by vegetation. Note the size of the tracks, how many toe prints there are and the distance between the tracks.
* **Look at the detail of the tracks**. Has the animal got long claws? Are its feet webbed? See if you can tell which tracks belong to the forefeet and which belong to the hind feet. Are there any other clues—feathers, hair or droppings? Have its wings or tail left their marks, too?
* **Watch for droppings**. Animals leave behind their own characteristic droppings. The droppings of a dog or fox are different from the small pellets that rabbits and deer leave behind. Look for owl pellets—oblong rolls of fur with tiny bones inside. After eating a mouse or vole, the owl coughs up the part of its meal that it cannot digest. Foxes sometimes do this, too.

MORE ABOUT MAINE

* Bears are not true hibernators but rather experience a period of physical dormancy, or winter sleep. With true hibernators, their body temperatures and heart rates drop drastically, while a bear's body temperature only drops a few degrees. True hibernators will urinate and defecate during their hibernation, while a bear does not.

* In the Penobscot version of the moose legend, Gluskabe did not downsize the moose before putting humans on earth because the moose showed humility and stated he had goodwill toward the newcomers.

Chapter 6

MAINE'S BOUNTY

Fall brings the harvest of two of Maine's classic crops. One of them readily comes to mind: apples, in all their luscious splendor. The other is less obvious but equally important. Autumn is also the time of the potato harvest, and the gleaning of this crop has been a huge part of Maine's agricultural history for generations. Growing potatoes is a major Maine industry, and up in "the County," site of the state's great potato farms, fall signals a call to the fields.

LIFE IN THE ORCHARD

On a crisp fall day, sounds of merriment fill the air as families clamber aboard a hay wagon, ready to head into the orchards for an afternoon of apple picking. Nothing says fall like the sweet tang of a fresh apple, and what better way to get some than to visit a Maine orchard and pick your own?

Apple farms are an integral part of New England's agricultural heritage, but running an orchard comes with its own set of challenges. Despite the difficulties, many of Maine's apple farms, such as this one in Limington, have survived for centuries.

Brackett Orchards is believed to be the oldest family-owned and operated orchard in Maine. The original founders, two brothers, settled Limington in 1783 after finishing stints in the Revolutionary War. Upon

Workers picking apples. *Photo by George French, courtesy of the Maine State Archives.*

clearing the land, they immediately planted apple trees. Today, Manley Brackett, ninety-one, is the eighth generation to run the orchard. He and his late wife, Virginia, ran the farm for many years, and now he works along with his daughter, Deborah, and son-in-law, Guy Paulin, to grow nine varieties of apples on 75 of the farm's 450 acres.

"We grow McIntoshes, Cortlands, Spencers, Macouns, Red and Gold Delicious, Empires, Paula Reds, Northern Spy and Honey Crisp," he says. "I grew up harvesting apples—it's all I've ever done. I started when I was six years old, picking up drops. If there's a category in the *Guinness Book of World Records* for harvesting the most apples, I may be a contender!"

Brackett says they keep the farm going because it is their home and way of life, but he admits running an orchard is not usually a moneymaking scenario. "It used to be, but now you're lucky to break even," he says. "And it's very challenging. In 2009, we lost a third of our apple crop when we had a late spring frost after the blossoms had set up. That hits you hard. Still, people know the name, Brackett Orchards; they know we offer a good product, and they come year after year to pick and to buy our apples and cider at our farm store. Part of the reason we keep going is because of them."

Guy Paulin, who runs the orchard day to day, agrees that the apple business can be tough. "Within the last seven or eight years, we have really been squeezed by imports, especially those from New Zealand," he says. "It used to be that people primarily bought the old favorites, but now they can go to the grocery store and find eighteen to twenty different varieties from all over the world. It can be hard to compete with that."

Still, Paulin is optimistic about the future and plans to keep the orchards going. "People around here love the farm and want it to continue," he says. "They like coming here and walking through the orchards, sitting on a farm tractor and seeing how the farm works. For many, it wouldn't be fall if they couldn't come to Brackett's and pick apples. The 'buy local' movement has also helped us, and we hope that continues."

Brackett's does grow other crops, including pumpkins, squash, blueberries and potatoes, and sells these items, along with jams, maple syrup and cider, at its farm store. Other than the pick-your-own efforts and hay rides, it has not offered any other tourist-type entertainment at the farm, but Paulin is thinking that the farm may need to evolve in order to survive.

"Manley has kept the store pretty traditional, and it's done well," he says. "But we may need to seize the opportunity and offer more items. If you have people come all the way out here to pick apples and visit the store, why not entice them to buy more by offering some additional Maine-made products? We may also look into other apple-based goods that we can develop and sell."

Maine orchards, like other farming enterprises, continuously face the challenges of managing costs, finding the right help and coping with bad weather. In addition, as Paulin alluded to, they must evaluate when it is time to make changes and what those changes might be.

As one farmer noted, if growers want to compete in today's market, they have to make changes. Today's farmers are not just competing with other local markets. They must also deal with a global economy, and expecting to farm as one did twenty years ago and survive is no longer realistic. Yet making changes in agriculture is hard, not just because it means changes to the land, but also because changes cannot be made overnight. If a farmer decides to grow new crops or new varieties, it takes time for them to come to a productive stage. Growers must allow for that and hope that the time, money and labor invested pays off.

Some orchards have switched from raising classic apple favorites such as Cortland and McIntosh apples to also growing cider apples and heirloom apples with names like Golden Russet, Wickson, Ashmead's Kernel,

Hudson's Golden Gem and many others. An apple raised for cider does not taste as good as a regular eating apple, but it is perfect for creating that golden liquid that is autumn's essence. Farmers who develop cider making as a significant part of their enterprise gain some insurance in case their crop of eating and cooking apples is damaged by storms or spring frost or some other unforeseen event. A cider apple crop is much more stable.

New England orchard growers have also been challenged by the fact that they are competing with apple farms from out West and overseas. McIntoshes and Cortlands were the region's premier apples for most of the twentieth century, but in recent years, that market has been undercut by the Red and Golden Delicious apples from the Northwest. Strong marketing campaigns, underwritten by big orchard cooperatives, have made inroads in a market that was once dominated by New England fruit. New shipping technology has also allowed apples to be successfully imported from other countries, with apples like the South African Granny Smith able to arrive in mint condition and gobble up even more market share.

"The Granny Smith was developed to be an export fruit, and it has done very well," says Paulin. "McIntoshes just don't hold up as well when it comes to shipping long distances. Factor in the lower labor costs involved in growing Granny Smiths, and smaller New England orchards can't compete."

Yet proactive orchards, such as Brackett's, are surviving. By diversifying their offerings and catering to the popularity of the "buy local" movement, they are able to carry on. As another farmer said, "We still grow McIntoshes and Cortlands—there will always be a market for them—but if we had not expanded our offerings, we would not be in business."

Most farms open their orchards for families to come and pick, as well as for visits by bus tour groups and school groups. A few have seen visits from inner-city schoolchildren who were amazed to discover that apples grew on trees. "To see their reaction after picking and tasting a fresh apple is priceless," said one farmer. "It makes being a grower worthwhile."

APPLE LAND

Most of Maine's apple orchards are in the southwestern and central part of the state. They flow from the Sanford area up through Lewiston and Auburn, Augusta and Waterville and on toward Bangor. Eighty-four farms, covering more than 2,000 acres, currently produce about one million bushels of Maine apples each year. The average Maine apple farm is about 20 acres, although there are some smaller than 1 acre, and the largest orchard spans 320 acres. In recent years, four Maine orchards have been certified organic in response to increasing interest in organically grown crops.

What makes good apple land? Acreage that has good air drainage—meaning that cold air flows away from the crop and does not "puddle down" and freeze. The soil should hold water well so growers rarely have to worry about drought. Interestingly, Maine's extremes of temperature are beneficial, as the cold snaps mixed with milder days make apples both hard and sweet.

In spring, Maine's apple land is covered with cloud-like blossoms of pink and white that billow in the soft breezes. Bees buzz continuously amidst the blossoms, and songbirds flit in and out, building nests and nurturing young. By late May, the blossoms have passed, and the trees are showing shiny green buds of fruit. The fruit swells and ripens under the lazy summer sun. By late August, the apples are close to harvest (earlier for some varieties), and come September, the season of the apple is in full swing. Pickers will work day and night to bring in the crops, although some will be left for the pick-your-own trade. Drops attract wildlife and insects, including yellow jackets and honeybees that buzz lazily on the fallen fruit, satiated by its juicy sweetness.

Although fall is when most people think of apples, the business of growing them goes on year-round. After the harvest is done, the pruning of hundreds to thousands of trees (depending on the size of the orchard) begins in December and runs until June. In April, farmers collect leaf and soil samples to evaluate the nutrients the trees might need. These are evaluated for phosphorus, nitrogen, magnesium, potassium and other key elements. The trees are then fertilized according to what is required.

Spring is the time of replanting and adding new varieties. More than one hundred varieties of apples are grown in Maine, with most farms growing twenty to thirty different types. Two varieties, the Black Oxford and the Brock, originated in Maine; both are known for having "balanced flavor and firm flesh" and are fine for eating and for baking in pies. The McIntosh remains the most commonly grown variety in New England and among the top ten most popular in the United States. This classic tree originated in the wilds of Ontario, Canada, more than two hundred years ago. John McIntosh so liked the crisp apple he found in the woods near his home that he propagated additional trees by grafting buds from the original onto rootstocks. The rest is history!

Each spring, most apple farms replant about 10 percent of their orchards. However, that does not mean that there is not an abundance of older trees.

There are trees on many farms that have been producing good fruit for a century or more. As any grower will tell you, apple trees are very hardy and quite capable of withstanding both harsh Maine winters and other onslaughts of nature.

Spring is one of the busiest times at an orchard, with most days typically starting at 5:00 a.m. Often, farmers work through the night, especially if rain is in the forecast. The window for fertilizing and spraying is short, and a long rainy spell can shrink that timetable even more.

The trees are sprayed for scab, a deadly fungus that can wipe out an entire orchard, and mowing in the orchard goes on from spring through fall. It is important to reduce long grass near the trees, as it can provide nests for mice and other potentially damaging wildlife.

July brings the first apple crop, and the harvest goes on through October, just in time for favorite fall foods such as apple pies, crisps, dowdies and more.

At the orchard, baskets and crates of shiny, red apples are everywhere, and their sweet scent permeates the farm stand. Cider and doughnuts are being sold, with the tang of the drink matching that of the autumn air. The last hay wagon rumbles back from the orchards, dispelling a group of tired but happy families with their bags of apple bounty. Such ends the day during apple season. "You can't do this job for money," says Manley Brackett. "You have to love it. You work seven days a week, twenty-four hours a day. You have to accept the changes of weather and of fate and realize that you will never be wealthy in money, but you will be rich in other ways."

Heirloom Apples

Ask people their favorite apple varieties and you are unlikely to hear "Pomme Grise" or "Esopus Spitzenberg," but long ago, these apples were popular. Today, a few orchards are growing heirloom varieties, and these old-fashioned apples with unusual names are once again attracting a following.

The Esopus Spitzenberg is one of those gaining fans, as it is a flavorful apple with a special connection to Thomas Jefferson, who raised it at Monticello. Reputed to be Jefferson's favorite apple, Esopus Spitzenberg was grown at Monticello when the variety was just getting established. It originated in the mid-1700s near Esopus, New York, in one of the many orchards planted by Low Dutch settlers. Esopus is sweet, tart and full of "complex fruity and spicy flavors," according to pomology journals. The apple is lovely in appearance, with hues of reddish orange cascading over yellow tones. It is harvested in late September to early October, but the apple's flavor is at its peak from October through December.

Here is a sampling of other returning favorites:

Golden Russet: This apple originated in the 1700s and was known to George Washington and his compatriots. A golden apple with an orange blush, it is sweet, aromatic, gently tart and quite lovely in appearance. It is prized for eating, cooking, cellar keeping and making hard cider. Golden Russets are typically harvested in mid-October and are at their flavor peak from October through February.

Wickson: This tiny apple with brilliant red and yellow skin was first developed in the 1800s for (hard) cider making. It was named for a distinguished California pomologist. The Wickson is tart and aromatic with "unique herbal and spicy flavors." It tastes great, but its small size left it often overlooked by commercial growers. Wicksons are harvested in early October and are at their flavor peak from October through December.

Ashmead's Kernel: This old English favorite is known for its sweet-tart spicy flavor. It was first introduced to North America in the 1700s. The Ashmead won many taste competitions in its native England, including several at the Royal Horticultural Society. Its color is striking—look for a copper to reddish gold apple. This variety is harvested in mid-October and at its peak from October through December.

Hudson's Golden Gem: Considered "strangely elegant," the Hudson's Golden Gem originated sometime in the 1930s. The story is that an apple seed dropped in an Oregon hedgerow produced the first Gem tree, and it was propagated by fans of the fruit ever since. It has an intensely sweet flavor and a "glowing complexion." The Golden Gem is harvested in early October and at peak quality from October through November.

Pomme Grise (Grey Apple): This little apple came to the United States from the St. Lawrence Valley in Canada, where it has been grown for more than 150 years for local and specialty markets. It has a sweet, nutty taste and may be related to an old French variety called Reinette Grise. If this is true, than the Pomme Grise captures a taste of King Louis XIV's time.

Calville Blanc d'Hiver: This French apple has long been a cook's favorite, having been grown for more than four hundred years. It has firm, white flesh and a tart, intense flavor. It is a bit unusual looking, with an irregular, lobed shape and smooth, bright green skin. Some think it looks like a little pumpkin, but it tastes great.

Cider: Autumn's Essence

Crisp and cold, it captures the sharp tang of autumn in a glass; warm and fragrant, it breathes the mellow sweetness of the season. Either way, cider distills autumn's essence. Authentic, old-fashioned cider is refreshing in a way that no other drink matches. The Shakers believed that the best cider making commenced when the air was chilly and the ripening fruit had a fragrance that could be noted "at thirty feet distance." With apples at their peak, they could be gathered, chopped and put through the press until the liquid gold flowed freely.

Cider is called "sweet cider" until it starts to ferment. While it still has a pleasant taste but tiny bubbles have formed, it is called "hard cider," which is slightly alcoholic. As fermentation progresses, it will transform into apple cider vinegar. Apple cider has also formed the base of many popular drinks, including apple champagne. This sparkling drink is created by adding equal parts brown and white sugar to apple juice and then allowing it to settle for eight weeks in a cool place. Old-timers sometimes made an apple brandy, called "apple jack," by leaving a bucket of hard cider outdoors once the nighttime temperatures dropped below freezing. The watery part of the cider turns to ice, leaving a stronger, more potent concoction behind.

Apple cider has long been a classic American drink. In colonial times, hard cider was found at nearly every table. John Adams is reported to have downed a tankard of hard cider every morning before breakfast—and he lived to age ninety-one! Ben Franklin was another regular imbiber. In 1840, William Henry Harrison made his devotion to hard cider part of his presidential campaign. Harrison was being denounced by supporters of incumbent Martin Van Buren as nothing but a rough frontiersman who was entitled to "no more than a soldier's pension, a log cabin and a barrel of cider." Rural Americans took offense to what they perceived as a rustic slur and formed their own "log cabin clubs," which served cider; others in Harrison's camp offered generous cups of hard cider to woo voters. The "cider campaign" worked, and Harrison was elected.

Many classic American recipes call for cider, including Pennsylvania Dutch spicy cider soup, apple butter, Shaker apple omelets with cider sauce, plus numerous options for simmering ham in cider or roasting pot roast in the same. Old-time recipes for mincemeat, meat glazes, doughnuts, pies and various punches and warm drinks frequently call for cider, sweet or hard.

Both horse- and man-powered cider mills were commonplace across rural America for many years, but today classic mills are hard to find. A popular one exists, however, in Eliot. King Tut's Cider Mill up on rural Goodwin Road has attracted a faithful following since 1903. The family has been raising apples and pressing cider for generations, and the press currently in operation dates from before the 1900s. Early photos show farmers bringing in their horse-drawn wagons full of apples to get their cider made; they would then leave with cider in fifty-gallon wooden barrels. Today, the wagons are gone, but the cider making continues.

Ken Tuttle epitomizes the classic Mainer; a burly man who favors flannel shirts, he sports a gray beard, ruddy cheeks and spectacles. A ball cap—de rigueur in Maine—adorns his head. He and his brother, Dennis, still work the family farm, harvesting apples from gnarled old trees and making their cider on the ancient press.

The cider is not pasteurized and has nothing added to it; it is liquid apple in its purest form. Because of the lack of pasteurization, it cannot be sold in stores, so those wanting "the real deal" must come to King Tut's to buy their taste of autumn. And come they do. Generations have bought cider from the Tuttles, and word has spread that here is cider at its purest. Every weekend through the fall, the Tuttles squeeze a fresh batch, and families flock into the little shop to see the old-fashioned press at work.

Ken jokes that the press was "state-of-the-art eleven decades ago," and he has a point. It is a mind-boggling contraption, full of plates and levers, chutes and pulleys. Seeing it in action causes jaws to drop in amazement. The Tuttles press a combination of apple varieties to make the tastiest cider and what they feel is a "healthy beverage." They choose McIntosh, Cortland, McCoun and Spencer for their blend. The apples are loaded onto a conveyor belt a half dozen at a time; the conveyor chugs up nearly to the ceiling of the old barn before dumping the apples into the grinder. The grinder, which creaks and groans with age, reduces the apples to mush. Ken explains that this soupy mix—very similar in appearance to applesauce—is what they call "pumice" or "pummy." Next, the pummy is poured into wooden trays, and Ken and Dennis spread the mixture by gloved hand until it is evenly dispersed. The trays are wrapped in cheesecloth, which acts as a filter, and then a wooden slat is placed on top. Once they have a tower of ten to twelve trays and slats, they are ready to press the apples.

The stack of trays and slats is rolled into the press; the old hydraulic pump is activated, pulleys are engaged and fifty tons of weight press down on the pummy, squeezing out the precious cider into a stainless steel vat. It takes one bushel of apples to make three gallons of cider. The cider will later be pumped into bottles, and the Tuttles will sell one pint, half gallons and gallons of cider.

A peek under the cheesecloth reveals a squished mess of apple seeds and skins, yet while the remains are not appetizing to look at, they will provide good fodder for pigs and other farm animals.

The Tuttles have worked at making and delivering cider since they were boys. Dennis recalls delivering cider on his bike at eight or nine years old and helping to wash out bottles. Today, he loves seeing families come to experience the art of cider making for the first time. He and Ken also eagerly greet longtime customers, many of them now elderly. "I have a number of older customers that I see every fall," says Ken. "They say my cider is the only thing that keeps them regular. As long as they drink this, they have no problems!"

King Tut's Cider Mill is in operation every weekend from Columbus Day to New Year's Day. You can come buy cider or bring your own apples to be pressed, which costs five dollars per gallon. The Tuttles prefer the cider made late in the fall, believing that the late apples have "gotten more sugar up," thus creating the sweetest blend. "The frost brings out the sugar and the flavor," says Dennis. "Early cider is made from mostly Macs, because they ripen soonest. Later, you have more apple varieties to add to the blend, which improves the flavor, and the cool temperatures give it that extra something special."

MORE ABOUT MAINE

KING TUT'S CIDER MILL
815 Goodwin Road (Route 101)
Eliot, Maine

Open weekends from Columbus Day
to New Year's Day
Saturday, 9:00 a.m. to 5:00 p.m.,
and Sunday 10:00 a.m. to 5:00 p.m.
(207) 439-5797

HOW TO MAKE YOUR OWN CIDER

Any kind of apples may be used, but experts prefer a mix of apples, including ones known for sweetness, ones known for tang and those with a nice aroma. If you use apples that have been left on the ground, your cider will have an earthy taste. Drops should also be checked for worms and other insects. Unripe apples will be too starchy for cider making.

Remember, it takes a bushel of apples to produce one to two gallons of cider.

After the apples have been picked, let them sit a day or so to bring up the juice and flavor. Next, scrub them and cut out worm holes or any decay. Be sure to keep the apples, your equipment and your work area clean. Equipment should be cleaned with detergent in between pressings of cider.

Before pressing the apples, grind, chop or crush them into a fine pulp. You can use a food processor, apple grater or slaw cutter.

For small amounts of cider, you can strain the apple pulp through a porous cloth bag with someone's help. You will need to periodically wring the juice out of the bag and into a tub or vat. For larger amounts of cider, you will need a press. Apple presses, both of the old-fashioned variety and more current models, are sold online through a range of independent sellers and farm stores. A quick Google search will yield various options. Up in Maine, a copy of *Uncle Henry's Swap or Sell It Guide*, a "we sell anything" catalogue, is also a good bet.

The apple juice caught in the tub or vat can be drunk immediately but tastes better if left to set for a few days. It is best to refrigerate the cider.

POTATOES—THE OTHER FALL CROP

A steaming bowl of whipped potatoes with butter melting into the whirled peaks, crispy fries paired with a burger, soft potato slices layered with melted cheese...mmm. Any way you serve them, potatoes make the dish. Few foods are as versatile and tasty, and Maine proudly harvests thousands of bushels of this popular crop each fall.

Maine ranks eighth in the nation in potato production, with more than sixty-three thousand acres under cultivation, primarily in the state's northernmost county of Aroostook. This sprawling, largely flat landscape has the right mix of cool temperatures and well-drained soils that potatoes love. In the 1940s, Maine led the nation in potato production, but increased competition from national and international markets has since changed the picture. While the longer growing seasons in other regions have enabled farmers in those areas to bring more potatoes to market, Maine farmers have hung on and found their niche. Today, they grow a number of potato products ranging from seed potatoes to specialty varieties whose uses range from potato chips to French fries, appetizers and more.

Down on the Farm

Albert Fitzpatrick of Houlton farms three hundred acres of potatoes. A farmer for forty-five years, he grew up in the business and then started his own spread at age twenty-one with just thirty acres. Today, he grows Russett Burbanks for McCain Foods, round whites for Frito Lay and a variety of reds and Yukon Golds for seed and table stock. "You have to be diversified with your crop in order to serve a variety of markets and reduce the risk of disease," he says. "If you farm just one crop and a contract falls through or a blight strikes, you could be wiped out."

Like most agriculture, potato farming is driven by the weather, and in Maine, you can go from sun to rain, warm to cold, in twenty-four hours. "The weather is the single biggest factor in whether we have a good season or not," says Fitzpatrick. "In 2011, I could not start planting until May 17; in 2010, I was done planting by May 15! If you have a rainy June or July, you can get water rot in the fields and lose much of your crop. It is always a bit of a gamble."

Typically, planting is done in early May, with farmers putting in twelve- to fourteen-hour days in order to get the crops in. "Ours is a short season, so we need every bit of growing time," says Fitzpatrick. "We plant as fast as we can and use every bit of daylight." They plant seed potatoes—either whole potatoes or ones that have been cut into three or four pieces by a special seed cutter. In June, the potatoes are hilled, a practice that will be repeated two or three more times as the potatoes grow. While efforts are being made to reduce the use of chemicals, most large-scale potato farmers find that they must spray for fungus and certain pests. "Potato blight, the disease that caused the Irish Potato Famine of the 1830s, is much less common but still a threat," says Fitzpatrick. "Because of that, and other similar diseases, we

Children dumping bushel baskets full of potatoes into empty barrels. *Photo by George French, courtesy of the Maine State Archives.*

Fall is the time of the potato harvest up in Aroostook County, known as "the County" to Mainers. This photo shows the harvest, circa late 1930s. *Photo courtesy Maine Potato Board.*

need to spray, especially if the weather is humid and wet. Fungus and mold thrive under those conditions."

By July, the fields are a carpet of blossoms, stretching to the horizon. Once the crop is mature, the farmers spray to kill the tops. For most market sectors, the fields are left alone for three weeks to allow the potatoes to set up skins. During this time, farmers check the crop periodically to see how things are progressing. "We have to kill the tops or the skins wouldn't set up," explains Fitzpatrick. "With skins on, you can store your crops for quite some time."

Fall brings the harvest, which typically runs from around September 10 to October 10. Days are long once again, and schools close in much of Aroostook County so older children can help harvest. Much of the harvesting is mechanized now, but teenagers aged sixteen or older can drive harvesters, and many hands are pressed into work to sort potatoes and pack them for the potato storage houses.

Darrell McCrum, a potato farmer from Mars Hill, says the harvest would be difficult without the teenagers' help. "It would take us a lot longer and cost a lot more to bring in the crop without them working," he says. "The kids also earn money for college this way, so it is good for them. Potato farming is part of our culture up here. By having the next generation involved, we keep young folks interested in farming."

As the potatoes come in, workers sort out rocks, debris and any potatoes of poor quality as the crop streams by on a conveyor belt. The potatoes must be carefully handled, as any bruising can break down their cells and allow fungus to get in. On a farm like Fitzpatrick's, as many as ninety thousand potatoes might be harvested in a season, with a typical yield of about three hundred one-hundred-weight bags to an acre.

The potatoes are stored in storage houses set to different temperatures. The ones Fitzpatrick has for McCain Foods are stored at forty-seven to forty-eight degrees Fahrenheit; his table stock and seed potatoes are at forty degrees, and his Frito Lay potatoes are at fifty-one degrees. The temperature will be constantly monitored, and cool air may be pumped in as needed. Potatoes can successfully store in the houses all winter long without air conditioning, which is one advantage that Maine farmers have. In the southern part of the country, potatoes must be processed as soon as harvested, so the crop has limited long-term storability.

Growing for the Future

Erica Fitzpatrick Peabody, Albert's daughter, is an agronomist with McCain Foods. She is part of a new generation that is creating a successful marriage between traditional farming skills and science. "We consistently try to improve a potato's quality and to make varieties more sustainable, more economical and more disease-resistant," she says. "At the same time, we are also always experimenting with new varieties so we can better serve different markets." Also involved in her family's farm, Peabody is excited about the natural breeding efforts that might one day yield more disease-resistant potatoes but knows it is a long process. "We have some promising products, but it could be ten years before we have enough seed to launch them commercially. We also have to educate the consumer about new varieties so they are encouraged to try them."

Despite the competition, Peabody believes that Maine potatoes will continue to command a good market share. "We have a lot of natural benefits when it comes to growing potatoes," she says. "We typically get adequate rainfall, so we don't have to irrigate; it is cold here in the winter, and that kills a lot of bugs and fungus, so we don't have to fumigate our soils. Our winter temperatures are cool, so we can store potatoes for a long time without the expense of air conditioning at that time of year, and we are blessed with rich soil. All of our farmers also rotate their crops, only growing

In the 1940s, Maine led the nation in potato production. *Photo courtesy Maine Potato Board.*

Potato harvesting in the earlier part of the twentieth century was very labor-intensive. Note the worker gathering the potatoes by hand and filling the barrels. Schools would close for weeks so that "all hands" could aid in the harvest. Today, the harvest is more mechanized, but schools still close or have a shorter period so that the crop gets in on time. *Photo courtesy Maine Potato Board.*

potatoes in one section every other year, then switching to a grain or grass crop like clover, so we keep nutrients in the ground."

Maine potato growers already supply potatoes to giant consumers such as McDonalds (one of the world's largest users of potatoes) through McCain's, and Peabody feels Maine is positioned just right for other key markets. "I think our position will continue to improve," she says. "As someone who grew up on a family farm, and as an agronomist, I am committed to growing high-quality potatoes—as we all are. Maine is also close to big markets on the East Coast. We have a big processing center for McCain here in Aroostook County and are close to the Frito Lay facility in Connecticut, plus a number of farmers have developed their own successful product lines. I think the future looks good."

McCrum is one of those farmers who runs a processing facility in Belfast and produces a product line, Penobscot McCrum, that ships to food outlets such as TGI Fridays. He sells twice-baked potatoes, potato skins and other potato products this way.

A fifth-generation potato farmer, he thinks the future looks good but also sees challenges ahead. "Increasingly, we have to compete in a global market,

A barrel of just-picked potatoes is readied for hoisting onto a truck. *Photo courtesy Maine Potato Board.*

so we need to educate the consumer about the value of locally grown goods and the wonderful varieties we have in our own backyards," says McCrum. "We also need to show people what it takes to grow food—I think there is somewhat of a disconnect when it comes to the consumer understanding the costs involved. When you understand the expenses a farmer faces, you realize that you are getting a good value."

McCrum's family has twenty-two kids in the next generation, and he feels there is a very good chance that some of them will continue with the farm. "Most of us don't want to do anything else," he says. "There's a freedom in farming that you do not get with any other line of work. The best way I can express it is it's in our blood; it's part of who we are, and that's why I feel there will always be potato farms in the County."

MORE ABOUT MAINE

Maine's Potato Blossom Festival

Celebrate the spud at the Maine Potato Blossom Festival held every July in Fort Fairfield. The annual event features a potato-picking contest, the Potato Blossom Queen pageant, Maine's longest parade, live music, road races, fireworks and family fun. For more information, visit www.fortfairfield.org or call (207) 472-3802.

The Super Tuber: Nutrition Facts

Potatoes often get a bad rap in terms of healthy eating, but in reality, they are highly nutritious foods. Toppings are the culprit.

Potatoes are excellent sources of potassium, vitamin C, iron, fiber and B6. To learn more about potato health benefits and for recipes, visit www.mainepotatoes.com.

Chapter 7

A Taste of Downeast

Autumn's bounty means plenty of good things to eat, and the crisp fall air certainly feeds one's appetite. Hearty casseroles, creamy chowders, baked beans, sweet pies warm from the oven—each captures the flavor of the season. Classic Maine dishes tend to be simple fare, the kind that has sustained generations of loggers, fishermen, lobstermen, farmers and others who work hard on land and sea. Because Mainers have always lived and worked so close to abundant natural resources, their traditional meals reflect the harvest close at hand.

Maine food also has its roots in a strong colonial heritage, with many items borrowed from Native American traditions or developed because they worked well when cooked on hearths. The fact that they tasted good, were easy to make from ingredients at hand and kept "body and soul together" ensured their enduring through the generations.

One Mainer's Heritage

Maine was first settled in 1623, along the shores of Kittery. I am proud to note that my ancestors were among those Piscataqua pioneers in the form of one George Fernald, a young surgeon in the British navy, who sailed up the aforementioned river, saw the stunning land before him and stayed. Generations later, my great-aunt Jessie Fernald was growing up in a small town on the river called Eliot. Born in 1886, she started baking breakfast biscuits for her father and nine siblings at the age of ten; she soon had a skilled hand at all forms of cooking, and a family legend was born.

I think of Auntie all the time, but fall brings special memories. I remember as a child running to her house after a walk in the woods and getting a slice of warm corn bread. Saturday nights the house would be fragrant with the smell of baked beans and fresh-baked apple pie for dessert. Holidays meant cranberry pudding with sauce so good you could lick the bowl. Her recipes were comforting and simple but heavenly to taste. Each mouthful made a memory as loving and sweet as she was.

I share some of her recipes with you here, as well as the stories behind some of Maine's classic fall foods.

"AUNTIE"

"Auntie," as she was known to one and all, stood barely five feet tall and never weighed one hundred pounds. She had a sweet, careworn face crowned with a cloud of snow-white hair. She wore simple black tie shoes and a plain cotton dress every day, with an apron tied on when she cooked.

Tiny as she was physically, there was no question that Auntie was a strong Maine woman. She grew up dirt poor on a farm where hard physical work was part of life. She dropped out of school at age sixteen to work as a maid/governess, thus providing income for her family. Over the years, she traveled the country, surviving flash floods, the San Francisco earthquake and fire, and she once killed a six-foot rattlesnake with a bullwhip. In the 1930s, she returned home to stay with her widowed sister and helped raise her sister's two children. By the time, I was born, she was well into her eighties yet still spry. I can see her holding a giant brown crockery bowl in the crook of one thin, wiry arm and, with the other hand, beating one hundred strokes a minute as she whipped batter into shape. I could not manage half that speed! But her real strength was of the spirit, the kind that overcomes, carries on and still finds joy in life.

Auntie's Apple Pie

Homemade Maine apple pies often have lumpy, browned crusts, the result of being packed with sweet apples. A pie that looks too perfect and manicured just does not say "homemade."

Apple pie is a fall classic almost everywhere, but especially in Maine, where orchards are abundant. Apple pie is a tradition at most Thanksgiving tables but is eaten as often as possible throughout the fall and winter. Serve it warm with a topping of vanilla ice cream or cold so the apples' tang is a bright burst of flavor in the mouth. Either way, it is delicious! It also comes highly recommended for breakfast.

This recipe is for a nine-inch, double-crust pie. It is best to prepare the bottom crust first, then the apples and then the top crust.

One tip on the crust: Auntie always said, "Don't be afraid of your dough." In other words, when shaping the dough into two balls, prior to rolling it out, do not hesitate to grab the dough firmly and use some oomph as you pack it tightly into a ball. Show the dough who is boss. When rolling, roll with vigor! This way, you maximize the use of your crust.

FOR THE CRUST

2 cups sifted, all-purpose flour
1 teaspoon salt
⅔ cup vegetable shortening
7 tablespoons of cold water (water is best if chilled in the fridge in advance)

Sift flour and salt together and then blend in shortening with a pastry blender until you have small pebbles of dough and shortening combined.

Sprinkle 1 to 4 tablespoons of water over half of the mixture, then toss the mixture with a fork until it "balls up." You can also use your hands to firm up the ball. Once one ball is formed, push it to one side and repeat the process with the other half of the dough.

Note: Sometimes, dough does not behave as it should—you may need to add more water to get the flour and shortening to stick together and form a ball; if you add more shortening, you must add more flour so the recipe stays in proportion.

Prior to rolling out the dough, wet your workspace with a wet cloth and leave it damp. Put down your wax paper over the damp surface. Sprinkle a teaspoon of flour on the wax paper and put down your first ball of dough. Sprinkle a bit more flour on top of the ball of dough. Top with another sheet of wax paper. Roll out the dough until flat; roll in all directions. Use your nine-inch pie plate as a guide to how big to roll out the dough. The crust should be bigger than the plate. Bring the plate up close to the dough and flip crust into plate, fitting it around the edges.

For the Filling

Six to eight good-sized apples (I like McIntosh, but some prefer Cortland), peeled, cored and cut into thin slices
¾ to 1 cup sugar
½ to 1 teaspoon ground cinnamon
Dash of nutmeg

Mix apples and spices together in a bowl. Once mixed, start layering them into the piecrust. It is best to place the thinnest slices around the outer edges and thicker slices in the center. Use more thin slices to fill in any odd spaces.

Spoon any extra of the sugar/spice mix over the apples. Place five dots of stick margarine on the apples—one on the top, bottom and each side and one in the center.

Fix the top crust per the instructions for the bottom crust and place over pie. Notch the edges together with a fork, and slice three openings in the center of the pie so it can vent. As Auntie would say, "No one wants a white-livered pie," so take a small cup of milk, dip your fingers in it and "paint the pie crust" here and there with milk to ensure browning. No need to cover the whole pie, just dab here and there and especially any patched places.

Bake your pie for 50 minutes at 450 degrees Fahrenheit.

Squash Pie

This recipe is for a nine-inch, one-crust pie.

Follow the same instructions for making crust as for apple pie, except roll out only one crust. Squash pie has no top crust. You may have extra dough but can use this to make Cinnamon Sticks (see later recipe).

½ cup of sugar
½ teaspoon salt
1 teaspoon ginger
½ teaspoon nutmeg
½ teaspoon cinnamon
*1 can squash pie filling**
2 eggs
1½ cups milk

Mix sugar, salt and spices. Blend well into the squash. Beat the two eggs separately. Add eggs and milk to the squash mixture, stirring well. Pour into a 9-inch pie plate already lined with crust. Make sure the crust is standing high, as this filling will fill the piecrust and then some. If you have extra filling, pour it into a ramekin or other small baking dish and bake it along with the pie as an extra pudding to have on the side.

Be sure your oven is preheated.

Bake the pie for 20 minutes at 425 degrees Fahrenheit, and then for 40 minutes at 375 degrees. Pie is done when a knife inserted into the center comes out cleanly.

*In Auntie's day, fresh squash would be used, but this involves a lot of chopping, mashing and occasional bad language. A can of pie filling works just fine.

Pumpkin Pie

This recipe is for a nine-inch, one-crust pie.

Follow the same instructions for making crust as in apple pie recipe, except roll out only one crust. Pumpkin pie has no top crust. Again, extra dough can be used to make Cinnamon Sticks.

1½ cups canned pumpkin
¾ cup sugar
1 teaspoon salt
1 to 1¼ teaspoons ground cinnamon
½ to 1 teaspoon ground ginger
¼ to ½ teaspoon ground nutmeg
¼ to ½ teaspoon ground cloves
3 eggs, slightly beaten
1¼ cups of milk
1 six-ounce can (⅔ cup) evaporated milk

Combine pumpkin, sugar, salt and spices. Blend in eggs, milk and evaporated milk. Pour into piecrust. Make sure the piecrust edges stand high because the filling will come right up to the top. Bake for 50 minutes at 400 degrees Fahrenheit or until a knife inserted into the center comes out clean.

Cinnamon Sticks (for Leftover Dough)

Roll out your leftover dough into strips—not too thin or they will burn up. Brush them with butter and then sprinkle on sugar and cinnamon to taste. Bake for roughly 10 to 15 minutes at whatever temperature the pie is at. You will need to check them, as ovens vary; also, a pie cooking at a hotter temperature will see the sticks ready sooner than a pie cooking at a lower temperature.

Apple Pan Dowdy

This old-time recipe is lovely in its simplicity. It also brings to mind the old song lyrics: "Shoo-fly pie and Apple Pan Dowdy makes your eyes light up and your stomach say 'howdy!'"

Bisquick or any quick-bake biscuit mix
8 medium-sized apples (I use McIntosh)
1 cup of water
2 inches of stick cinnamon
¼ cup of sugar
Dash of mace
1 pint light or all-purpose cream

For the Biscuit
Make biscuits according to package instructions. You may also substitute any classic strawberry shortcake biscuit recipe.

For the Applesauce
Pare, quarter and peel 8 medium apples. Combine apples and ¼ to ½ cup of water and 2 inches of stick cinnamon. Cover and simmer until very tender, about 10 minutes. Remove cinnamon. Mash apples until smooth and stir in ¼ cup of sugar. NOTE: Mace may be added with the stick cinnamon while apples are simmering, or it may be added after apples have cooked, when you add the sugar.

Serve dowdy while biscuits and applesauce are warm; cut biscuits to individual serving size, top generously with apple sauce and pour cold cream over all to taste. Dowdy biscuits and applesauce will microwave fine when you want to reheat them. (Add cream *after* microwaving.)

Maine Cranberries

In fall, the fruit that first comes to mind is the apple, but there is another red, glossy crop that is also ready for harvest when autumn arrives. Cranberries are ripe and ready for picking come September, and while you will not sit on the porch munching one (unless you want all the saliva to leave your mouth), these tart berries add incredible flavor to many fall and winter recipes.

Cranberries are most closely linked with Massachusetts, specifically the Cape Cod region, but Maine has a healthy cranberry industry as well. As of 2010, more than thirty cranberry farms operated in Maine. Cranberries are related to blueberries, and while they are grown in many parts of the state, the bulk of them are raised in Washington County, which is also the site of the famed blueberry barrens. Cranberries like acidic sandy or peat-type soils, as well as boggy sites. Maine's cool climate, chilly nights and good rainfall also provide good growing conditions for the berries.

Cranberries are found in the wild, and Native Americans picked them for use in food, medicines and dyes. In 1816, the first cranberries were grown commercially in Dennis, Massachusetts, and the industry grew from there.

Cranberries grow from April to November, with harvesting beginning in September. In cranberry country, the streams literally run red, as the cranberries are floated free for gathering. This harvesting technique has led to the misunderstanding that cranberries grow in water, but they actually grow on vines that sprout from low-growing evergreen shrubs. Some of these shrubs might live to be 150 years old or more, so cranberry growers rarely have to replant.

Cranberries are harvested when the berries turn red. The berries have pockets of air inside of them, so they will float. Thanks to this unique characteristic, most cranberries in the United States are "wet-picked," or floated from their vines. Cranberry bogs are flooded with six to eight inches of water, and water-reel harvesters, called "egg beaters," are used to stir up the water, dislodging the berries from the vines. The berries float to the surface, and wooden or plastic booms are then used to corral them. Once grouped together, the berries are removed from the water either by conveyor or pumped into a truck. They are then taken to a receiving station for cleaning, sorting and freezing. Wet-harvested cranberries are used for juices, sauces, sweetened dried cranberries and as ingredients in other food products or nutrition items.

Some farms do both wet-picking and dry-picking. Dry-picking is more labor-intensive and does not have as high a yield, but fruit harvested this way is less apt to be bruised and is usually marked for the fresh fruit market (as opposed to being frozen). With dry-harvesting, farmers use walk-behind machines that comb the berries off the vines and into burlap bags. Bog vehicles or helicopters then remove the berries from the fields. At the receiving stations, the fruit is graded and screened based on color and its ability to bounce. That's right—a good bounce is indicative of a fresh, firm berry! A soft cranberry will not bounce.

Cranberries slated to be sold fresh are stored in shallow bins or boxes with perforations or slatted bottoms that allow for air circulation. Because cranberries are harvested in cool northern climates, they can be stored in thick-walled barns without refrigeration. Opening and closing barn vents is all that is needed to keep the berries at the right temperature until they are sold.

Cranberry beds may be flooded again during the winter to protect against cold temperatures. In Maine, this winter flooding will turn to ice, and once that forms, trucks can be driven onto the ice to spread a layer of sand. The sand will help control pests and rejuvenate the cranberry vines. Sanding is usually done every three to five years.

Maine's oldest cranberry farm is Bradshaw's in Dennysville, about thirty miles from the New Brunswick border. Bradshaw's started in 1991 with just one-quarter of an acre under cultivation. Today, five acres are planted. The farm claims its berries are "nourished by the mist and fog of the Dennys River and the Hardscrabble Stream, which feeds into Cobscook Bay." Bradshaw's runs its harvest September through November and has fresh berries for sale from October through mid-November. In addition to berries, it sells fruit spread and sauce.

Cranberries are face-puckering tart by themselves but blessed with health benefits. They are loaded with vitamin C and antioxidants and are recommended for promoting oral health, healthy urinary tracts and an overall good constitution. With just a touch of sweetener, they are the perfect addition to breads, cakes, muffins, puddings, cookies, pies, pancakes, chicken, cheese balls and more.

Auntie's Steamed Cranberry Pudding and Gorgeous Sauce

This pudding showcases cranberries in all their glory. The pudding has a delightful kick thanks to the berries' tartness, while the sweetness of the sauce is the perfect counterpoint.

Cranberry Pudding

2 teaspoons of baking soda
½ cup of molasses
½ cup boiling water
1½ cup sifted flour
Pinch of salt
1 teaspoon baking powder
1 cup cranberries (fresh or frozen; if frozen, thaw before using)

You will need a one-quart mold; you can make do with a greased coffee can.

Add soda to molasses and mix together. Add boiling water, stirring as you pour it in. Next, add sifted dry ingredients. Toss cranberries in a little flour to coat them and then mix in with the batter.

Pour the batter into the greased mold. Cover the mold with saran wrap or foil. Steam for two hours. Serve warm with Gorgeous Sauce.

Gorgeous Sauce

½ cup cream
½ cup sugar
¼ cup butter

Put ingredients in the top of a double boiler. Bring the water in the boiler to a boil and stir mixture until a creamy, yellow sauce forms. Serve the pudding with warm sauce on top.

Store leftover sauce in the refrigerator; stir to re-blend. Pudding may be stored in foil. Both can be reheated in the microwave.

Note: Auntie often served this pudding for holidays. She would make the pudding itself a day ahead to save time.

The New England Making of Marshmallow Fluff

Paul Revere's great-great-great-granddaughter Emma Curtis of Melrose, Massachusetts, is credited as being the originator of the fluffernutter (although her sandwich was not initially called that)—the now classic sandwich featuring peanut butter and Marshmallow Fluff. But where did Marshmallow Fluff come from? In New England, it is a time-honored treat, but many other parts of the country have never heard of it.

Curtis and her brother, Armory, first began making a marshmallow crème called Snowflake Marshmallow Crème in 1913. (The Curtises did not invent marshmallow crème—several other companies sold something similar—but they were extremely successful in advertising their product.) Emma printed up recipes and distributed them in brochures and in a newspaper column; she also later promoted them on radio and television. During World War I, she published a recipe for a peanut butter and marshmallow crème sandwich, which she christened the "Liberty Sandwich." It was very popular, but that successful debut was only the beginning. A few years later, the Curtises launched SMAC Marshmallow Fluff and printed the Liberty Sandwich recipe on the label. With such exposure, the sandwich's combination of sweet and nutty tastes quickly garnered legions of fans across New England—and boosted sales of Fluff in the process.

Emma Curtis died in 1948, but her brother ran the company until 1962. The company folded when a fire destroyed its marshmallow factory.

Meanwhile, over in Somerville, Massachusetts, Archibald Query had also been making marshmallow crème in the years prior to the first World War. When the World War I sugar shortage hit, Query's business foundered, and he wound up selling it for $500 to two veterans, Allen Durkee and Fred Mower of Swampscott. Fresh from France, they decided to call Query's crème "Toot Sweet Marshmallow Fluff." The pun did not catch on, and their product soon became known simply as Marshmallow Fluff. The rest, at least in New England, is history.

Durkee-Mower promoted Marshmallow Fluff aggressively, sponsoring and creating radio shows, recipe books and, finally, the fluffernutter sandwich. The combination popularized in Emma's Liberty Sandwich was officially dubbed the fluffernutter in 1960, when Durkee-Mower's advertising agency came up with the name. It is now a term uniquely New England.

So what is in Marshmallow Fluff? Sugar syrup, corn syrup, vanilla flavor and egg whites—a combination New England cooks, and generations of kids, greatly appreciate.

Baked Apples with Marshmallow Fluff

6 large apples
1 cup brown sugar
1 cup water
2 tablespoons butter
½ teaspoon ground cinnamon
½ teaspoon ground nutmeg
Marshmallow Fluff to taste

Core 6 large baking apples and pare a strip from around the top of each. Place in a large baking dish.

Combine brown sugar, water, butter and spices in a saucepan and bring to a boil, stirring as it heats. Pour hot syrup around apples.

Fill the center of apples with Marshmallow Fluff.

Bake apples uncovered at 350 degrees Fahrenheit for about 45 minutes.

CLASSIC INDIAN PUDDING

Indian pudding is a uniquely American dish that historians have traced back to the seventeenth century. It is believed that the dish has its roots in England's hasty pudding, a porridge made by stirring boiling milk or water with wheat flour. The colonists did not have ready access to wheat flour, but they did have plenty of cornmeal, or "Indian meal," as it was sometimes called. They also had an abundance of molasses, which was being produced in tremendous amounts thanks to the demand for rum. During Boston's booming rum trade of the seventeenth and eighteenth centuries, molasses was available as an inexpensive sweetener, and so many old-time recipes call for its use. Indian pudding was frequently cooked alongside baked beans, another Maine staple.

Indian pudding is baked for a fairly lengthy time at a low temperature. This form of cooking was typical of early New England kitchens, where the hearth was the center of the home. "Low and slow" cooking not only created great dishes, but it also kept a home warm for hours.

Indian pudding is not the most attractive dish in terms of appearance—basically, it is brown, lumpy custard. However, it does have a special appeal. The mouth-watering scent of spices permeates the home as it bakes, and when served, its comforting warmth combined with those old-fashioned flavors creates a most pleasing dessert. Indian pudding served hot with a dollop of cold vanilla ice cream is called "Heaven 'n' Hell," but one bite definitely puts it in the angelic realm!

Indian Pudding

3 cups of milk
⅔ cup dark molasses
⅔ cup yellow cornmeal
⅓ cup sugar
1 teaspoon salt
¼ teaspoon of cinnamon
¼ teaspoon of nutmeg
¼ cup butter or stick margarine
1 cup milk

Heat oven to 300 degrees Fahrenheit. Grease a two-quart casserole dish. Heat 3 cups of milk and the molasses, stirring frequently to blend. Do not let the milk scald. Mix together the cornmeal, sugar, salt, cinnamon and nutmeg. Gradually stir these dry ingredients into the hot milk mixture. Add the butter. Continue to cook over low heat, stirring constantly until thickened. This will take at least 10 minutes.

Once thickened, pour into casserole dish. Pour 1 cup of milk over the pudding just prior to baking. Do not stir it into pudding. Bake for 3 hours, uncovered.

Note: With my oven, I found that 2.5 hours uncovered works best. You may need to gauge actual baking time based on your own oven's performance.

Serve hot with vanilla ice cream, cold cream or fresh whipped cream.

SATURDAY NIGHT STAPLE: BAKED BEANS

Baked beans are what is for dinner on Saturday night in New England. They may be served with sausages, hot dogs, ham, scalloped potatoes, home fries, cole slaw or rolls, but throughout the fall and winter months, beans are a suppertime staple.

Baked beans became a Saturday night tradition because they could cook all day Saturday, be eaten Saturday night and then be reheated on Sunday for another meal. This allowed cooks to rest on the Sabbath. Many Mainers added another layer to the tradition by opting for beans for Sunday breakfast or cold bean sandwiches for lunch.

Baked beans are also traditional fare at Saturday night church suppers. From September through May, the Congregational Church in Eliot, Maine, hosts a ham and bean supper one Saturday night every month. Huge bowls of steaming baked beans are brought to each long table, where people dine family style. While the beans are being passed around, platters of cold cuts arrive, followed by huge casserole dishes filled with scalloped potatoes, hot rolls, cole slaw and lots of hot coffee. Dessert—if you have room—is homemade pie, available in a variety of tempting options, baked by the church ladies. The open kitchen allows for plenty of banter back and forth between the male and female cooks as guests come and go. People from all denominations, as well as out-of-town visitors, flock to suppers like these, knowing that they will be able to eat their fill of tasty, hearty food while enjoying good company.

Baked beans originated with Native Americans four centuries ago; they baked their beans in earthenware pots. Today, classic baked beans are still baked in crockery bean pots.

Some people bake their beans with bits of onion or bacon; others stir in a spoonful of sweet maple syrup (this can also be done after the beans are baked), but the classic New England recipe calls for molasses.

Once cooked, the flavor of baked beans can be enhanced with a number of embellishments. Purists may opt for pickle relish or mustard, but ketchup is also popular.

Auntie's Baked Beans

Soak beans overnight in cold water. Either kidney (red beans) or pea beans (navy beans) may be used, although you would cook each kind separately. To start, parboil the beans (bring to a boil) in baking soda and water until slightly tender. Drain but save the liquid. Put beans in a classic crockery bean pot with salt pork that has been slightly cooked; that is, cooked until grease starts to form. Add 3 tablespoons of molasses, ½ teaspoon of dry mustard and 1½ teaspoons of salt. Return the liquid to the beans and make sure they are covered with water.

Bake covered at 400 degrees Fahrenheit for about 1 hour. Then reduce the heat to 350 degrees for 2 hours. Reduce heat to 325 degrees for the rest of the baking time—approximately 5 hours. You will need to check the beans periodically to see when they are done (it could be sooner). Beans should be soft but not mushy and must not be allowed to go dry. Total cooking time is usually 8 hours (from the 400-degree stage through to the end). Add boiling water as needed. Remove the cover on the beans for the last half hour if you like.

Steamed Brown Bread (the Classic Accompaniment to Baked Beans)

1 cup rye flour or standard flour
1 cup corn meal
1 cup whole wheat flour
2 teaspoons of soda
1 teaspoon of salt
2 cups of buttermilk or soured milk
¾ cup molasses

You will need a 1-pound greased mold (a greased coffee can will do).

Mix dry ingredients. Stir in milk and molasses. Beat well. Fill the greased mold two-thirds full. Lay waxed paper over the top and steam in a steamer for 3 hours. Serve piping hot with butter.

Bean-Hole Baked Beans

Bean-hole baked beans, or beans cooked in a hole in the ground, are legendary in Maine. They, too, originated with Native Americans but were soon adopted by the settlers and became a particular favorite at logging camps. Today, you can still enjoy bean-hole baked beans at a number of events throughout Maine, including Harvestfest in October in York and as part of Maine Living History Days, also held in October, at the Maine Forest and Logging Museum at Leonard's Mills in Bradley. Bean-hole baked beans are also frequently offered at dozens of church and community suppers throughout Maine, so check local newspapers.

Bean-hole baked beans have developed a certain mystique, but basically, what allows the beans to cook this way is the crockpot principal. A bean-hole pit maintains a low but constant cooking temperature over a long period of time. The beans will ultimately be fully cooked but not burned.

Bean-hole beans in the making. The hole has been dug and prepped with coals. Here, the men are lowering the kettle, filled with beans, into the hole. Next, it will be covered with more coals, and the beans will cook all night. *Photo courtesy First Parish Church of York, Maine.*

The instructions outlined here are meant to be more descriptive of the process as opposed to step-by-step guidelines. For really good "how-to" information, any Google search will yield not only articles but also videos on how to do bean-hole beans.

What sets bean-hole beans apart is the fire pit, which is usually three feet wide by three feet deep but can vary in size depending on how large the cooking pot is or how many pots of beans are being cooked at a time. The pit is filled with dry firewood and set ablaze—which is why large-scale bean-hole cooking in a number of towns is often done by the fire department. Dried hardwood is used, as it will produce long-lasting coals. Wood is added until the pit is two-thirds filled with coals. Now, it is time to add the beans, which should already be pre-soaked and prepared according to any number of favorite recipes.

Most bean-hole baked bean recipes call for the beans to be placed inside a Dutch oven. The old-fashioned version—and the kind to be used here—is made of cast iron with a tight-fitting, rimmed lid. The thick iron of the oven keeps the beans from burning, while the rimmed lid makes the container airtight and allows the beans to cook from the top down, as well as from the bottom up. (The oven will not only sit in the coals, but it will also have coals heaped on top of it.) The beans will cook anywhere from five to eight hours, or as old-timers say, "Until they're done." Removing the beans from the bean hole takes some skill and usually involves various homemade but tried-and-true contraptions made of coat hangers, chains and other elements since the bean pot is too hot to touch and the coals must also be avoided.

Recommended beans for the bean-hole method include old-time varieties such as Jacob's Cattle, Yellow-Eye, Great Northern, pea beans and Soldier Beans.

Simple Corn Bread

1¼ cups all-purpose flour
¼ cup corn meal
¼ cup sugar
2 teaspoons baking powder
½ teaspoon salt
1 cup skim milk
¼ cup vegetable oil
2 egg whites or 1 egg beaten

Heat oven to 400 degrees Fahrenheit. Grease an 8-inch or 9-inch pan. Combine dry ingredients and then stir in milk, vegetable oil and eggs. Mix until dry ingredients are just moistened. Pour the batter into the greased pan. Bake for 20 to 25 minutes or until the bread is light golden brown and a toothpick comes out clean when inserted in the middle.

Corn bread is a great accompaniment to soups, stews, chilis and chowders. Serve it warm with butter. Corn bread with real maple syrup poured on top is another old-time combination that is tasty as a snack or for breakfast.

New England Clam Chowder

¼ cup diced bacon
¼ cup minced onion
1 can (10.5 ounces) frozen condensed cream of potato soup
OR 1 can (10.5 ounces) condensed cream of potato soup
¼ cup milk
2 cans (7 to 10 ounces each) minced clams
1 tablespoon lemon juice
⅛ teaspoon pepper

In a large saucepan, cook and stir bacon and onion until bacon is crisp and onion is tender. Stir in soup and milk. Heat through, stirring occasionally. Stir in clams (with liquid), lemon juice and pepper. Heat through.

BRINGING IN THE CATCH

The state of Maine is practically synonymous with fishing, and seafood is a major part of Maine recipes, but the Atlantic's bounty comes at a price.

Many Maine fishermen are still putting out to sea in the late fall and winter. Fishing is a hazardous way to make a living at any time of year, but especially in late autumn, when the gales of the approaching winter are already roaring across the Atlantic. This time of year, fishermen have to go farther out, as fish head for deeper waters when winter approaches. The rewards can be significant, but the risks are greatly increased as boats are farther from help if they get into trouble, and the cold, turbulent waters of the Atlantic are unforgiving.

The catch they seek may be cod, haddock or flounder. The crews will work nearly around the clock with only short breaks from hauling nets, gutting and sorting the catch and then loading the fish into laundry-type baskets, which are lowered into the fish hold. In the hold, the fish will be stored in layers and put on ice. With luck, they will haul in nets full of fish and repeat the entire exhausting process at least four times a day. The fishing trip itself will last anywhere from a week to ten days depending on the weather. The crew will then have some down time before heading back out.

As autumn deepens, running into a bout of bad weather is almost a given. Many days, the crew are wet and frozen as they work in rain, wind or freezing spray. Rough seas can have waves splashing over the decks, adding to the misery—and the danger. Rogue waves can come out of nowhere, rearing up fifteen to twenty feet or more and sweeping men off the boat and into the churning ocean. Even more ominous are the days of strange calm, when the seas are a flat, mirrored gray and the sun shines palely in an overcast sky. Fishermen know that this kind of day is usually a weather-breeder and that somewhere, out beyond the horizon, is trouble in the form of howling winds and towering seas. They watch "the glass," the barometer that is their window on approaching storms, and prepare to batten down. Everything they have labored for is stored in the hold. For many, this catch is how they will pay their bills in the months to come. They will fight like hell to make sure the Atlantic does not get it back.

Even if a boat makes it safely to shore, storms can still do damage. Stormy weather makes it too rough to fish. Nets cannot drag well, lines cannot be set, gear is swept from decks and the risk becomes too great for boats and men. Nonetheless, as soon as the weather turns the least bit favorable, out they will go again—out to the deep seas and limitless horizon that has drawn Maine men for centuries.

Note: According to the U.S. Department of Labor's Bureau of Labor Statistics, commercial fishermen have a twenty-eight times greater risk of fatalities on the job then any other occupation. Commercial fishing is the United States' most hazardous occupation.

Baked Haddock

2.5 pounds of haddock is usually enough for four people (recommend skinned filets)
Milk
½ cup breadcrumbs or smashed Ritz crackers
¼ teaspoon salt
¼ cup margarine, melted
Lemon wedges

Only buy fresh fish; fish that smells "fishy" is not fresh. Many Mainers feel the best way to eat fish is as simply as possible. Fresh fish has plenty of flavor, and a light touch when preparing it is enough to create a satisfying dish.

At noontime, or early afternoon, rinse fish in cold water and then place it in a glass casserole dish. Fill the dish with milk—enough to cover the fish. Place fish and milk in the fridge to soak until dinnertime.

For a 5:00 p.m. supper, turn the oven on at 4:30 p.m. in order to allow time for the oven to reach a 500-degree-Fahrenheit temperature in time.

Remove fish from fridge and drain off milk, but do not rinse off fish.

In a pie plate, place ½ cup of breadcrumbs and the salt. Dip the fish in this mixture until covered on both sides.

Place fish in a fresh glass casserole dish that has been lightly sprayed with a non-stick cooking spray, such as Pam.

Drizzle ¼ cup melted stick margarine over fish.

Bake the haddock for 12 minutes at 500 degrees. Serve with fresh lemon wedges.

Hickory Nut Brittle

If a fall woodland walk brings you a good gathering of hickory nuts, try this sweet brittle.

¾ cup chopped hickory nuts
1 cup white sugar
½ cup brown sugar, firmly packed
¼ cup light corn syrup
½ cup water
2 tablespoons butter
Pinch of baking soda
Pinch of salt

Warm nuts in a 275-degree-Fahrenheit oven. Combine white and brown sugars, corn syrup and water in a medium saucepan and stir over low heat until sugar dissolves. Raise heat and cook without stirring until a candy thermometer registers 300 to 310 degrees or until drops thread when falling from a spoon. Remove the pan from stove, add butter, soda salt and the warmed nuts. Stir the mixture as little as possible. Turn at once out onto a buttered baking sheet. Quickly press candy into a thin layer with a spatula. When cool enough to handle, grasp edges with fingers, lift and stretch to make sheet as thin as possible. When cold, crack into irregular pieces.

*Recipe courtesy *Wildlife's Holiday Album* (National Wildlife Federation, 1976)

Chapter 8

Season's End

The November days are dwindling, the month fading as surely as the daylight. Drizzle takes on an icy cast, and the trees are nearly leafless. A few stubborn holdouts cling to the oaks and elms, rustling in the chilly winds that increasingly come from the east.

The harvest is in, and the tourists have long gone home. Homes are made snug and tight for winter. Snow blowers are primed and ready. Ice Melt is on hand, and shovels stand near the door. Already, warmer layers of clothing are required, for the November sun is feeble at best.

Deer have retreated deeper into the woods, seeking thick groves of evergreens in which to yard up for the winter while avoiding the last pursuit of hunters. Bear and woodchucks have gone to sleep, and only the squirrels appear with any regularity. Mornings are silent save for the cheerful gabble of the chickadees and nuthatches or the squawk of a jay.

As autumn winds down, the whole world seems to be in a state of waiting—waiting for that inevitable moment that signals the denouement of one season and the arrival of the next.

It happens late one gray afternoon. The temperature slides down a few critical degrees, and the first snow drifts down from the heavens. It starts as scattered flurries, a few flakes to catch on the tongue or watch melt on the fence rail. But as night closes in, the snowfall becomes steadier, and the fall landscape disappears under a mantle of white. The outdoor world is hushed amidst the falling snow, seemingly unaware that with this one storm, autumn has truly passed and the world has softly slid from one season to the next.

Bibliography

Armstrong, Charles. "Cranberry Fact Sheet." University of Maine Cooperative Extension Service.

Autumn in Maine Foliage Tours. Maine Tourism Association flyer, n.d.

Bennett, Dough, and Tim Tiner. *The Wild Woods Guide*. New York: Harper Resources, 2003.

Bruchart, Joseph, and Jonathan London. *Thirteen Moons on Turtle's Back*. N.p.: Philomel Books, 1992.

Burt, William H., and Richard P. Gressenheiden. *A Field Guide to the Mammals*. Boston: Houghton Mifflin ,1976.

Cromwell, Cathy. "Garden Guru: Howard Dill." www.garden.org.

Damariscotta Pumpkinfest. www.damariscottapumpkinfest.org.

Dotter, Earl. "Winter Harvest of Danger: Fishing on Board a Maine Trawler in the Storm-Tossed North Atlantic." Public Health Reports, July–August 2002.

Forever Locked! www.foreverlockedmoose.com.

Fryeburg Fair Program of Events, 2013.

Hook, Patrick. *North American Birds*. N.p.: Chartwell Books, 2011.

"How Cranberries Grow: Cranberries 101." www.cranberries.org.

Jacques, Shirley. "Sweet Time of Year: Eliot Man Keeps Up Family Legacy of Hand-Pressed Cider." *Foster's Daily Democrat, November 16, 2009*

Kabler, Jane. "Cranberries Are Used in Many Recipes." *Ledger Independent*, December 2013.

Kent, Crystal Ward. *Mainely Kids: A Guide to Family Fun in Southern Maine*. N.p.: University Press of New England, 2005.

Langevin, Don. *How-to-Grow World Class Giant Pumpkins*. Norton, MA: Annedawn Publishing, 1993. [Also see his blog, www.backyardgardener.com/wcgp/tips/10 steps.html.]

Maine Hunting & Trapping: The Official 2013–2014 State of Maine Hunting and Trapping Laws & Rules, produced by Maine Department of Inland Fisheries & Wildlife.

Maine Potato Board Consumer Information. www.mainepotatoes.com.

Maine State Pomological Society. Fact Sheet.

Miller, Howard E., and H.E. Jacques. *How to Know the Trees*. N.p.: William C. Brown Publishers, 1978.

Mount Agamenticus Conservation Region. www.agamenticus.org.

New England Historical Society. "The Revolutionary Roots of the Fluffernutter Sandwich." www.newenglandhistoricalsociety.com.

Peterson, Roger Tory. *A Field Guide to the Birds*. Boston: Houghton Mifflin, 1947.

Semour, Tom. "Lumberman's Legacy: Bean Hole Beans." *Fisherman's Voice*, August 2011.

WCSH Channel 6. *Bill Green's Maine Visits King Tut's Cider Mill, November 3, 2013*

Weiss, Laura B. "Looks Aren't Everything: An Ode to Indian Pudding." *Saveur*, November 2012.

Wildlife's Holiday Album. National Wildlife Federation, 1978.

"Wild Turkey." www.wikipedia.com.

UMaine. www.umainebeta.org.

About the Author

Crystal Ward Kent is a native Mainer and author whose work covers many genres. After studying journalism and wildlife ecology in college, she worked for the Maine Tourism Association for seven years, a stint that gave her extensive knowledge about the state she loves. Kent is also passionate about nature education and has developed a wide range of educational materials, programs and exhibits to help others understand and appreciate our natural resources.

Kent's work has regularly appeared in magazines such as *Taste of the Seacoast*, *Northeast Flavor*, *Coastal Home*, *University of New Hampshire Magazine*, *Bay State Builder*, *Granite State Builder*, *Yankee* and others. She has also written for the *Chicken Soup* books and *Guideposts* books and is the author of *Mainely Kids: A Guide to Family Fun in Southern Maine*. Her first children's book, *Tugboat River Rescue*, came out in 2012 and tells the true story of a tugboat rescue on the Piscataqua River. Her second children's book, *The Bad Cats of Biddeford*, will be out in 2014. She makes her home in Eliot, Maine.